CW01333655

TWO CENTURIES OF SHOEMAKING:
Start-rite
1792-1992

TWO CENTURIES OF SHOEMAKING:
Start-rite
1792-1992

KEN HOLMES

Published in 1992 by
Start-rite Shoes Ltd.
Crome Road
Norwich NR3 4RD

Copyright © Start-rite Shoes Ltd.

ISBN 0 9518888 0 3

Contents

Introduction — 8
Start-rite, 1792–1992 — 8
Leaders for 200 years and their dates at the helm — 13

Start-rite in history — 16
Industrial Norwich — 17
The shoe trade — 18
Ready-made shoes a godsend for Norwich people — 22
James Smith, leather seller and shoemaker — 25
Charles Winter, a man of outstanding ability — 27
The partnership of Willis and Southall — 33
James Southall takes over — 34
Export trade with the Colonies lost — 39
The firm gets a new Guv'nor — 41
James Laffan Hanly — 44

Start-rite children's shoes — 48
Patent — 48
The creation of the Start-rite company — 50
The nationwide survey — 50
How the new Start-rite shoe differed — 53
A nationwide fitting service — 54
By Royal Appointment — 58

Trade around the world — 59
Exports — 59
Sustained growth in France — 62
Into retail — 64
The growth of instock trading — 71
Employees remember — 72
A classic advertisement — 78

The home of Start-rite   82
    Where it all began   82
    The new Factory   84

Modern times   89
    The 1950s, a decade of change   89
    Start-rite bucks the industry's downward trend   91
    The boom years   94
    Cut-back   96
    The young board takes over   98
    A time for important decisions   105
    Meeting the challenge ahead   107

Acknowledgements

Many people have helped to provide information and check the facts for this publication, most of all the chairman, directors, and past and present members of the staff of Start-rite Shoes.

The author is also grateful to Mr John Dennis of Cromer for his painstaking research into the Winter family of which he is a descendant; to David Jones, Keeper of the Bridewell Museum of local industries in Norwich; the reference department of the County Library Service in Norwich for much useful information, but also to the reference departments at Manchester, Sheffield, Worcester and Gloucester, and the library and picture library of Eastern Counties Newspapers.

Books consulted which would provide much more information on aspects just touched upon in this history of one firm include *Norwich in the Nineteenth Century*, edited by Christopher Barringer, and published 1984 by Giddon Books; *Norwich: A Social Study* by C. B. Hawkins (published 1910); *The Story of Shoemaking in Norwich*, by W. L. Sparks, published in 1949 by The National Institution of the Boot and Shoe Industry; and *Trades and Industries of Norwich*, by Joyce Gurney-Read, published by Giddon Books.

Introduction

Start-rite, 1792–1992

The story of Start-rite Shoes of Norwich, the oldest footwear manufacturing company in England, embraces not only the history of Britain's shoe industry, but also that of Norwich industry since the Industrial Revolution.

Set up in 1792 by James Smith, this Norwich company has been producing footwear in times of war and peace, and boom and slump, without any break, for 200 years. The survival and continued prosperity of what is still a family firm is an outstanding achievement by any criterion.

It has been the result of dedicated leadership over the last two centuries by a number of remarkable men. They managed not only to keep 800 to 900 people employed in what was always a tough, highly competitive industry, but for the most part they also found the time to take a leading role in the well-being of the industry nationally, and to make notable contributions to the civic affairs of Norwich.

Certainly in the case of Start-rite, where family succession at the helm can be traced unquestionably from James Smith right down to the present day, sons, nephews and relatives by marriage have been responsible throughout for the continued prosperity of the business.

The most vital duty of the leader of a business, particularly a family one, is in selecting the right people to work with him. Almost any other business mistake can be rectified, but choosing the wrong colleagues can be disastrous. At Start-rite there has been a recurrent talent for selecting capable, hard-working men and women.

It still continues today at a time when the whole of British industry is hard pressed, and large sections of the footwear industry have been unable to compete against subsidised imports, and have closed down. Happily, the quality, stylish, fitting footwear produced by Start-rite, and the service given to their customers, is as much in demand as ever.

Readers should note that for some time it was thought that Start-rite was the oldest shoe manufacturing business in the British Isles, and it was recorded as such in *The Guinness Book of Records*. It has since been discovered that the honour in fact belongs to the Saxone Shoe Company's unit at Kilmarnock, now part of the Burlington International Group. It was in 1783, nine years before James Smith, that a shoemaker named George Clark opened the factory that was to become Saxone.

But Start-rite remains the oldest shoe manufacturing business in England, and is unchallenged in its proud record of remaining a privately-owned, family business.

The Bicentennial logotype.

David White, Start-rite chairman since 1978 photographed beside the portrait of Charles Winter, the founder's grandson, who ran the firm from 1827 until his death in 1867 and established the large factory business employing 900. People comment on a family likeness between the two.

Charles Winter's portrait was by John Clover (1779-1853), a Norfolk painter who exhibited at the Royal Academy from 1816 to 1836, and was a member of the Norwich Society founded by John Crome and Robert Ladbrooke.

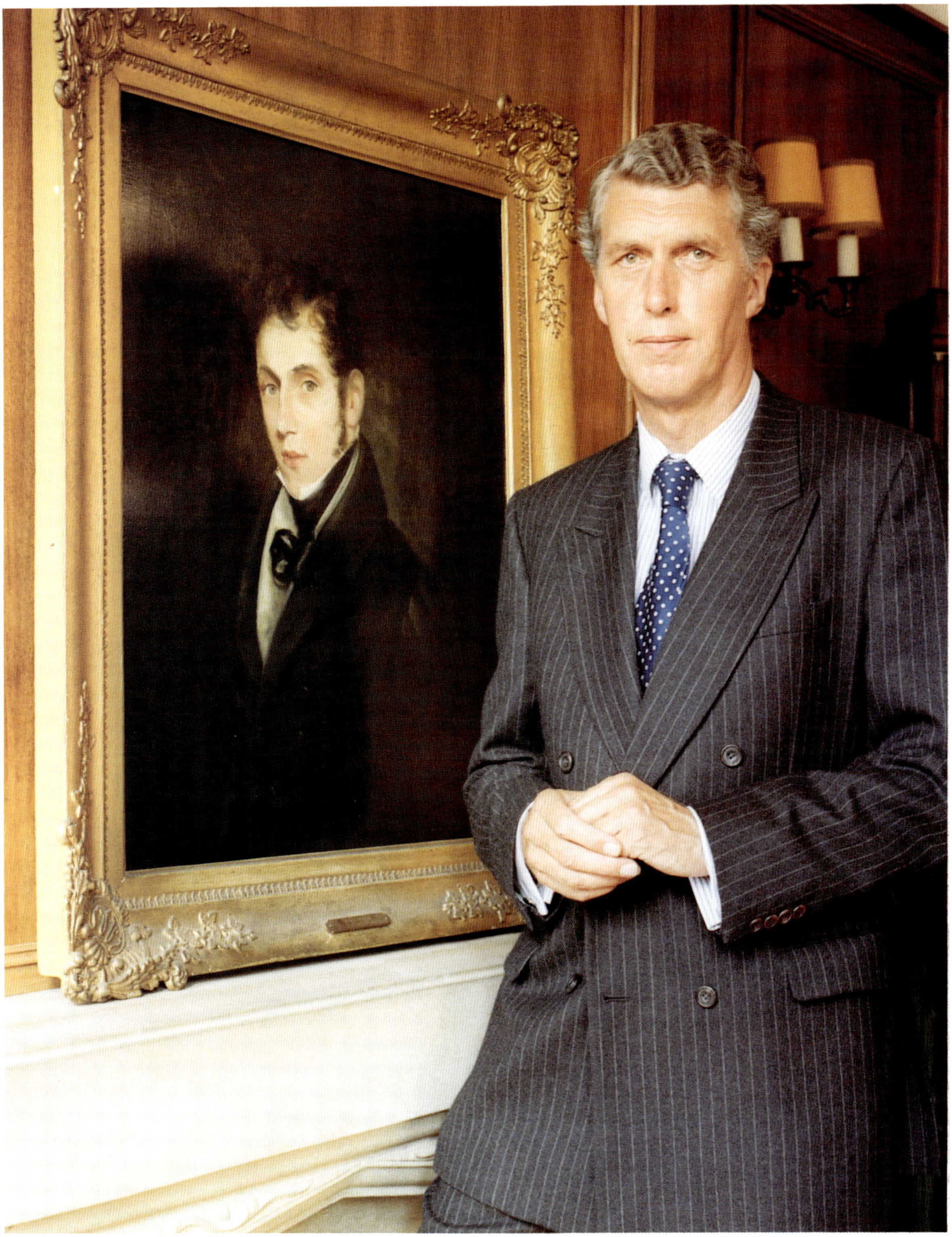

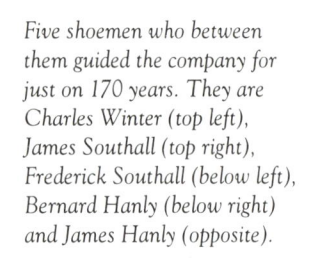

Five shoemen who between them guided the company for just on 170 years. They are Charles Winter (top left), James Southall (top right), Frederick Southall (below left), Bernard Hanly (below right) and James Hanly (opposite).

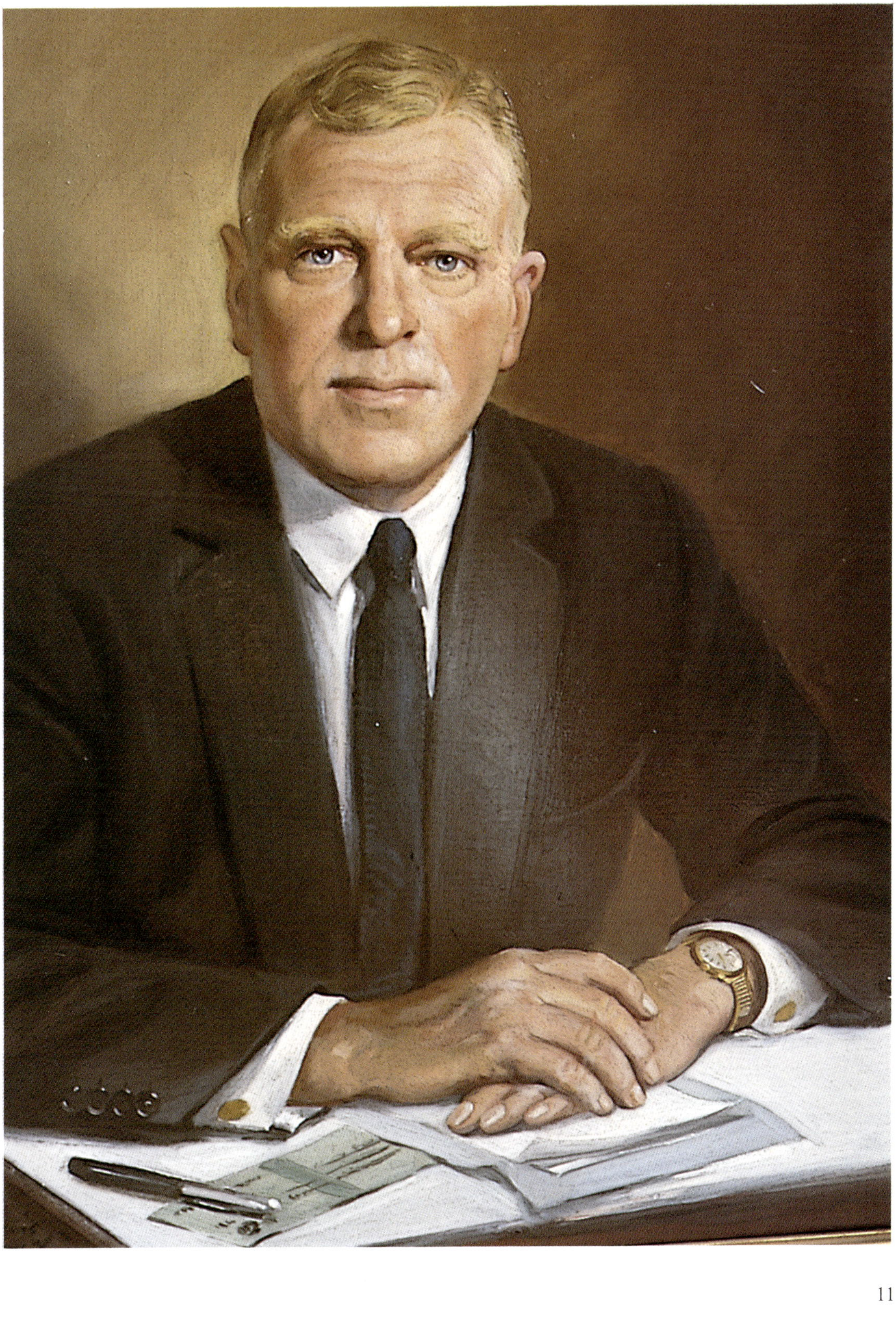

The picture (above) by David Hodgson of the Norwich School, hangs in the chairman's office. The building second on the right is the frontage of the factory developed by Charles Winter off St Peter's Street.

A staff outing, probably early in the 1900s. Among those seated are James Southall, his sons Charles and Frederick and, second left, the young Bernard Hanly.

Leaders for 200 years and their dates at the helm

1792—1818, James Smith   Born about 1762, James Smith was a travelling leather seller until he opened a shop where he made and sold shoes in the Upper Market, Norwich (St Peter's Street), according to Norwich land tax records.

He had a son Charles, and a daughter Mary Ann (1785—1820), who married William Winter (1783—1811). William Winter was described in his obituary in the *Norfolk Chronicle* of June 1811 as a shoemaker of Upper Market, aged twenty-eight, but no business link with his father-in-law James Smith is mentioned.

William Winter and his wife had three children, Charles, who was born in 1806, Mary Elizabeth and Sarah Hannah. It was Sarah Hannah's daughter, Marianne Wells who became the second wife of James Southall and thus ensured the family link with the business.

1818—20, Charles Smith   According once again to the city land tax records Charles Smith appears to have succeeded his father in carrying on the business for a short time, but he died in 1820. In her will his mother specified that if her grandson Charles Winter (then aged fourteen) was over eighteen but under twenty-one at her death, he was to be given the opportunity of carrying on the business of shoemaker in her shop and premises, but with trustees until he was twenty-one.

1820—27   Records show land tax payments on the St Peter's Street premises by Charles Smith's executors during this period.

1827—67, Charles Winter   This was a period of strong leadership and considerable growth when the large factory business was established.

Charles Winter's will left the business to be offered for sale in whole or in part to his son Charles Smith Winter, or wound up. C. S. Winter died in March 1867, aged twenty-seven, just two months after his father. C. S. Winter was referred to as a shoe manufacturer, so he appears to have taken the business on.

1868—88, Willis and Southall   In about 1860, it is recorded, the young James Southall came from London to work in the substantial factory of Charles Winter, presumably in a managerial capacity. A widower, he married his employer's niece, Marianne, seven years later.

It is a matter of conjecture, but almost certainly correct, that in order to take over the business, even then employing more than 700 people, fresh capital was needed. This was forthcoming from John Willis, a member of a Gloucestershire shoemaking family, who, two years after setting up Willis & Southall, married Mary Esther, the only sister of J. J. Colman of mustard fame. John Willis died in 1888.

TWO CENTURIES OF SHOEMAKING: START-RITE 1792-1992

INTRODUCTION

Changes in the form of exhibition stands — 1902 closed (top left) and 1980s open (below left).

1888—1920, James Southall Proprietor, and then first chairman of private company, James Southall & Co., registered 24 May 1900.

1920—26, Frederick Southall Chairman, son of James Southall.

1927—42, Bernard Hanly Chairman, son-in-law of James Southall.

1943—85, James Hanly Chairman, son of Bernard Hanly. In March 1966 James Southall & Co. became the parent company of Start-rite Shoes, with James Hanly remaining chairman of both companies until 1978 when he resigned as chairman of Start-rite Shoes.

1978—David White Grandson of Bernard Hanly, chairman of Start-rite Shoes. In 1985 David White also became chairman of James Southall & Co. on the death of James Hanly.

Today—Two of the eighth generation of descendants of James Smith now hold executive positions within the company. They are Peter Cross, senior multiple sales manager, and Peter Lamble, financial director.

Start-rite in history

During the research and reading carried out into the 200 years of history of the firm begun by James Smith in 1792, nothing came up to suggest that the centenary was marked in any way in 1892. James Southall may not have been the kind of man to take a backward glance and celebrate a remarkable century of endeavour. And understandably, with the death of Bernard Hanly in the 150th year of the firm in 1942, during the darkest days of the war, followed the next day by the death of the principal shareholder Fred Southall, there was little outward recognition of this milestone either.

Perhaps that is the reason why the 175th anniversary in 1967 was given more prominence than is usually associated with that timespan. It included a dinner in Norwich for customers, and a civic reception at which a gift of a 300-piece canteen of silver cutlery bearing the city arms was presented to the Lord Mayor of the time, Mrs Jessie Griffiths.

James Hanly, with his twin sisters Miss Joy Hanly and Mrs Catherine White, present silver cutlery to the Lord Mayor of Norwich Mrs Jessie Griffiths for the city's use to mark the firm's 175th anniversary.

The menu card for the dinner was cleverly designed to illustrate some of the tremendous happenings in the world during the lifetime of the firm. Starting with Nelson's victory at Trafalgar in 1805, the cartoon went on to illustrate the war of 1812–14 with the United States, the Stockton to Darlington Railway (1825), the sixty-four-year reign of Queen Victoria, the Great Exhibition of 1851, and the first successful transatlantic telephone cable in 1866.

This is followed by in 1875, Britain's half-share in the Suez Canal; the flight of the first aeroplane in 1903; the name Start-rite first used in 1921; the atomic bomb in 1945; the accession of Queen Elizabeth II in 1952; the end of rationing of food in 1954; the loss of Suez in 1956; the first man in space in 1961; and, no doubt to pinpoint the chairman's interest, although hardly on quite the same scale of importance, Norwich City beating Manchester United in the FA Cup in 1967.

The temptation must have existed, but it was probably decided against because many of the guests were from other parts of Britain, to have depicted the event as marking a significant contribution by the firm to local social and industrial history. That is what Start-rite is really justified in claiming.

Industrial Norwich

In 1792, when James Smith opened his shop to sell the fine, ready-to-wear ladies' shoes he was making, Norwich was on the threshold of change in its long-established pattern of trade.

Since the fourteenth century at least the looms had always been busy, bringing long periods of prosperity from a staple industry that had skilled workers able to spin and weave an abundance of local raw material into eagerly sought-after cloth. Flemish weavers and, later, French Protestants, all seeking religious tolerance, settled in Norwich, bringing with them not only their skills, but new ideas, and different techniques such as the use of silk as well as wool, or mixtures of the two, which brought new life to the staple industry. A visitor to Norwich in 1771 wrote of its notable crêpes and camlets, greatly in demand as exports, which brought to the city an annual trade of £$1\frac{1}{2}$ million — an enormous sum of money in those days. That prosperity, however, was coming to an end.

At that time Norwich had a population of 36,000, and was the third biggest town in the kingdom. Then came the introduction of steam power to drive the looms, and with coal available cheaply in the North, Norwich found it could no longer compete in the mass market. A further significant factor in the decline of the Norwich weaving industry was that its tradesmen chose to ignore fashion changes and the growing demands for different cloths.

Land enclosures, improved methods of cultivation and the use of machinery by farmers were also leading to unemployment in the countryside, so that during the early part of the nineteenth century the drift into the city from the rural areas swelled the Norwich population to over 50,000 by 1821.

In the city, as in the countryside, there were also signs of change. The cottage industries, where small family units, perhaps employing a journeyman or two, and apprentices, would work at or from home in a variety of occupations, were being challenged by the small factories. It was not a quickly changing situation, but continued for much of the nineteenth century.

Gradually, home weaving or shoemaking was to prove less efficient, and therefore less rewarding all round than the factories emerging behind the shop, or the wool and silk mills which were able to call on an abundant supply of cheap labour keen to work, and uncomplaining about long hours.

The first half of the nineteenth century in Norwich belonged to the entrepreneurs, not the landed gentry but a new breed of businessmen, motivated by ambition and self-interest, but not devoid of social conscience, who were to change the whole pattern of life locally. Colman, Jarrold, Bignold, Barnard, Copeman, Bullard and many others who are household names locally, first became known for their enterprise and business initiative in the early to mid 1800s. The hundreds of jobs created by Charles Winter's initiative in the middle of the nineteenth century through his development of his maternal grandfather's business must also have been a most worthwhile contribution to the local economy.

Further, Winter and many of this new genre of businessmen were also concerned with the social welfare of their fellow citizens. Through taking part in local government, and many of them exercising their strong religious convictions, they worked to improve the living standards of the people in the rapidly growing city.

The shoe trade

On taking a closer look at the shoe manufacturing business founded by James Smith, and carried on by his relations and able employees in succeeding generations, it is heartbreaking to discover how few detailed records remain. Shoes are worn and discarded, and although the shoemaker manages sometimes to keep a few of his favourite samples tucked away in the cupboard somewhere, his mind is always on the next range of shoes he is going to produce, or even the one after that.

He is seldom a man with a sense of history who files the drawings of his designers and retains them, keeps the swatches of his leather buyers, puts his outmoded machinery in a museum, or sets down the details of his daily transactions in the manner of a Parson Woodforde. It is those outside the

The Bridewell Museum, Norwich has on show machinery used in Norwich shoe factories in the nineteenth century. Seen here is: a press for cutting soles made by J. Collins (Norwich) c.1875.

TWO CENTURIES OF SHOEMAKING: START-RITE 1792-1992

A Blake sole sewing machine developed from a US patent of 1858 (opposite), and an early and later version of Singer treadle sewing machines.

industry who have painstakingly collected, for example in the Northampton Museum and the Bridewell Museum in Norwich, records of local shoe industries.

Before the Southall and Start-rite company records of this century, there is precious little written information available about the firm, and what exactly they made, and where or how they sold it, apart from one or two catalogues, and occasional newspaper and magazine articles, more usually dealing with people rather than their products or business.

There is, however, no reason to suppose that throughout the first century or more of its 200 years in existence, the firm departed from the generally competitive pattern of shoemaking, namely to supply what the public demands. Norwich was known for making fashionable women's shoes, slippers for men and women, and children's shoes.

Nobody has written with more authority and knowledge of the Norwich shoe trade than Wilfred Sparks, the former Sexton, Son & Everard production executive. His treatise for the fellowship of the National Institution of the Boot and Shoe Industry, published in 1949, has a unique blend of scholarship and practical knowledge.

Ready-made shoes a godsend for Norwich people

In the fifteenth century The Walk was known as Cordwainers' Row, and earlier than that White Lion Street was Saddlegate. Then there is the church of St Peter de Parmentergate in the area where the parmenters or leather sellers traded. There were master shoemakers, but they were small businesses employing the family, one or two journeymen, and apprentices, and working by the rules of the Cordwainers' Guild.

Leather was plentiful in this agricultural region, and even in the Middle Ages leather shoes were worn rather than the wooden clogs favoured in the North and on the Continent. For the better off, shoe styles changed often and their footwear was lavishly adorned and colourful, with red being a favourite colour.

The monstrosities which have found favour from time to time in recent footwear fashion, such as the platforms of the early 1970s, are not new. Pointed toes, high heels, fabric shoes, embroidery, buckles and other lavish adornments have all been seen before. The greatest change has been in the scientific construction of lasts and the improved fit of well-made shoes.

The cordwainer had to alter lasts to suit the shape and measurements of his customer's foot, and quite often these lasts were straight pieces of wood, not much resembling a foot at all. He took a great pride in his work, and undoubtedly derived pleasure from making a complete shoe. However, the writing was on the wall for this satisfying way of life when, at the end of the eighteenth century, James Smith began offering his ready-made shoes.

This was the beginning of an industry which increasingly became a godsend for the working people of Norwich as the nineteenth century progressed, and for much of the twentieth century was its staple industry, employing directly upwards of 10,000 people and creating many ancillary jobs. Now, as the twenty-first century approaches, it is still a significant contributor to the much-depleted local industrial base, despite the problems of unfair cheap imports of shoes.

Sparks speculates that James Smith had his own last sizes, basing them on the decree of Edward II that three barleycorns equalled 1in, and thirty-nine placed end to end equalled 13in, or the longest normal foot-size 13. He offers no explanation of what the girth measurement of a shoe, $\frac{1}{4}$in from size to size, was based on.

All that can be said with any certainty is that Smith found ready-mades profitable. He was able to take advantage of the manipulative skills of the under-employed weavers and turned out well-made, light, attractive shoes from the best of leathers, thus setting the standard from which the Norwich industry has departed at its peril ever since.

The problems of the Norwich weavers grew in the first half of the nineteenth century with the loss of much overseas trade through the wars, but

Charles Winter, grandson-by-marriage of James Smith, prospered. Much of the shoe trade then remained in the hands of the garret-masters who cut the uppers (clicking), and the 'bottom stuff' (soles, heels, linings, etc.). The uppers would usually be hand-sewn by women, and then passed out to other men working at home to be lasted. Winter must have organised some or all of these processes systematically in his expanding factory at the back of the shop in Upper Market, but also took advantage of the competition there was for work to be done at home. It was the coming of machinery, first the sewing machine, which swung the pendulum firmly in favour of factory work, and signalled the eventual demise of the garret-master.

By about 1840 the demand for ready-made shoes had become substantial. Charles Winter is recognised as the first manufacturer in Norwich to use the sewing machine for closing uppers in about 1856. By 1860 it is recorded that Thomas, Singer and Howes hand-sewing machines were used at the factory, then at Nos 7, 8, and 9 Upper Market.

One straight-sewing machine is said to have been capable of producing 3,000 stitches a minute, a performance which no way could be matched by hand sewing. Machinery for other shoemaking processes followed, and was soon under trial by the enterprising Charles Winter. Writers of the time mention the excitement caused by the appearance of the Lufkin folding machine, the Amazeen skiving machine (reputed to do in an hour what normally took the hand-operative a whole day), Wheel and Wilson's closing machine, Singer's binder and Singer's new rapid machine.

It became more and more difficult for the cordwainer and garret-master to compete, except as a source of cheap labour carrying out different operations and not making the whole shoe. Factory work, augmented by outworkers, who could be employed or not according to the state of the orderbook, was dominant by the mid-nineteenth century. During the 1860s between 800 and 900 workers were employed by Charles Winter in the factory and working at home.

Remarkably, a catalogue from 1871 survives. By this time the firm had become known as Willis & Southall, but such was his reputation that five years after his death the new proprietors described their business as 'late Chas. Winter'. In the catalogue they thanked their friends for the sustained and increasing commands with which they were favoured. This tradition is still carried on at Start-rite today, where it is not uncommon for customers to be regarded as friends.

The Willis & Southall catalogue recorded with pride the fact that, although perhaps the oldest house in the trade, their goods never commanded a more active demand than at that time. To meet this every improvement in machinery was promptly adopted.

The catalogue, illustrated by line drawings of the footwear offered, contained an almost bewildering variety of styles of ladies' shoes, children's shoes, ladies' and children's boots, slippers for men, women and children, and men's and youths' boots, both sewn and pegged, and riveted and machine-sewn.

In all, this fifty-four-page catalogue, printed by Fletcher & Son of Norwich, lists almost 1,000 different styles of footwear, as well as leggings, uppers for the trade, and large stocks from the firm's leather and shoe mercery departments. Approved makes of sewing machines could be supplied at manufacturers' prices.

Around this period, other manufacturers were becoming established in shoe manufacturing in Norwich, and large businesses such as Howlett & White and Haldenstein, and by the turn of the century the Sextons and other firms, were well on the way to becoming names known in the industry well outside Norwich. In 1900 between 7,000 and 8,000 men and women earned their living from shoemaking in Norwich, of whom 4,000 worked in factories.

Social surveys of the time showed that the factory workers were generally better off than the homeworkers, though they still worked from 7am to 7pm in the factories and earned little by present-day expectations and living standards. One factor which led to the shortening of factory hours was the realisation that it was asking a lot of operatives wishing to progress in their jobs also to attend technical classes late in the evenings.

David Jones, keeper of social history at Norwich's Bridewell Museum, says in his informative pamphlet on the Norwich shoe trade through the ages that a mid-eighteenth-century trade card showed that London makers supplied shoes that were available in their shops or could be supplied and sent to all parts of the country.

While some doubt must be cast on giving all the credit to James Smith as being the first person to supply ready-made shoes, there can be little doubt that, bracketed with the undoubted organisational ability of Charles Winter, the retail shoe trade in the provinces owes a great deal to the pioneers of the business now called Start-rite.

James Smith should be credited with setting the whole pattern of the future Norwich industry by making light, stylish shoes of quality, with the best leather and skilled labour.

While some might recall that there have been periods when certain Norwich manufacturers made cheaper shoes in order to sell to buyers at the price they would pay, 'Norwich Quality' is something that to this day the handful of surviving Norwich manufacturers guard zealously. To achieve it requires the use of the best available materials, the application of skill to the latest scientific techniques, the latest sophisticated machinery and highly trained operatives who have to carry out a hundred or more intricate operations to make a shoe that is both attractive to the eye, fits properly and will also stand up to everyday wear.

For much of the two centuries of the firm, the turnshoe was one of the main methods of construction used to make light shoes and slippers. There was a turnshoe department at Crome Road, which was still operating in 1949, Sparks noting in his publication when writing about Southalls, 'It is one of the few remaining shoe factories where one can still see turnshoes being made — in these days on the team system.'

Over the years, under the different proprietors and company chairmen and their various production experts, the constantly changing methods of mass shoemaking have been tried, and if suitable for use on high-grade leathers and the maintenance of quality, have been adopted. Machine sewing began to replace the constantly rising cost of turnshoe making during the 1920s, and in some methods of construction the bonding of sole and upper by sewing was replaced by the use of adhesives.

One of the most significant changes in manufacturing techniques in recent years has been the use of heated chambers to dry the leather on the last, giving a considerable saving in time and in the number of lasts needed.

Improved methods of lasting, the shoe without a single nail, and now computer-assisted manufacture, have all been employed to keep the firm competitive, with the important proviso that change can never be at the expense of being able to produce high-quality footwear.

James Smith, leather seller and shoemaker

Beyond the fact that James Smith started the business we now know as Start-rite in the Upper Market, Norwich in 1792, very little is recorded about him.

A diligent search of the history of the early days of making shoes in the mass in factory conditions, provides very little of the personal story of James Smith, and there is no contemporary newspaper record.

Over many years, writers about the shoe industry locally and nationally have stated that when this former leather seller opened his shop in the Upper Market in 1792 he stated that the system of making shoes to measure for each person 'made men dilatory', and that it was much better to manufacture a range of standard sizes and sell ready-made shoes from a shop.

Despite the fact that the boots for Cromwell's army were produced in Northampton without the individual soldiers being measured, and there are in existence trade cards showing that London makers could supply ready-made shoes in the mid-eighteenth century we like to attribute to James Smith a leading part in the development of the vast business of shoe retailing.

James Smith is far from the ideal name for genealogical or antiquarian research. Norwich land tax payments show that he opened a shop for selling shoes that he made on the premises at the Upper Market in 1792 on the site where the Norwich City Hall now stands.

The next recorded evidence of his existence is this advertisement from the *Norfolk Chronicle* of 14 May 1803:

'No. 9, Upper Market Street, J. Smith, Ladies Shoemaker. Returns his sincere thanks to his friends and ladies of Norwich and Norfolk for the very liberal support he has experienced since his residence in Norwich, and assures them that every effort in his power shall be exerted to merit their future favours.

'Notwithstanding the much advanced price of leather he is happy to say, from having connections with some of the first manufactories of leather in London he has it in his power to supply them on his usual low terms. NB. The trade supplied with kid skins, fancy upper leathers, and Turners incomparable blacking cakes wholesale.'

The phrase 'since his residence in Norwich' indicates that James Smith was not a native of the city, and because of his 'connections with some of the finest manufactories of leather in London' he may well have been a Londoner brought up in the leather trade who sold leather in and around Norwich before starting up his own business there.

There was no railway link between Norwich and London until 1845, so the leather sold by James Smith would have had a laborious journey from London by sea and river, or if it came by land it probably entered Norwich through St Stephen's Gateway. Much of the old city walls, and many of the gates were still standing when James Smith opened his shop and began making shoes in what was later known as St Peter's Street, in 1792. But they were in bad repair and did not escape demolition for long.

In more ways than one it was a time of change. For more than 500 years Norwich had never been without the clatter of looms. At the end of the fourteenth century there was a large settlement of Flemish weavers, with a second settlement at the end of the sixteenth century, and their skills in the weaving of mixed woollen and silk fabrics, and dyeing processes led to prosperity in and around Norwich. Towards the end of the seventeenth century French Protestant weavers also sought refuge in the city bringing in a new industry based on silk.

The good times continued until the latter part of the eighteenth century, when the Industrial Revolution, dependent on the cheap and plentiful iron and coal in the North, gathered pace while the textile industry of Norwich gradually declined, causing untold hardship, poverty and squalor among a great many skilled workers.

C. B. Hawkins, in his social study of Norwich published in 1910, says that for two and perhaps three decades early in the nineteenth century half the population of Norwich must have been in a chronic state of semi-starvation. They were crowded ten or more in a room in unsanitary conditions.

The work which James Smith and his successor Charles Smith were able to offer must have been most welcome at that time. They were fortunately able to tap a supply of labour with inherent skills and endowed with the lightness and nimbleness of hand required to make the finer kinds of footwear for which Norwich was to become famous.

When James Smith put up his trade sign in 1792, times were changing, with the upheavals of the French and Industrial Revolutions in the air, Thomas Paine publishing his *Rights of Man*, and years of industrial stability in East Anglia based on food production and weaving becoming less secure.

As often happens in stirring times, there was a drastic break from the past in women's dress. Bustles, paniers and corsets were abandoned for high-waisted Empire gowns of light muslin and calico. Exquisitely crafted shoes complemented the Neo-Classical look.

At the end of the eighteenth century kid leather rather than cloth began to be the fashionable material for women's shoes. Ruched ribbons and fancy buckles replaced ostentatious buckles on the dainty shoes which the slightly shorter skirts allowed to be seen occasionally.

Toes were either pointed or oval shaped. The court fashions of 1790, which the London connections of James Smith might have hastened to Norwich, required light shoes with needlepoint toes. The low, curved Italian heel was both elegant and practical.

What is reasonably certain is that in meeting the needs of the fashionable, better-off ladies of Norwich right in the centre of the town, and also in supplying the softer, superior grades of leathers to the many shoemakers — who probably averaged about one to every two hundred of the population of the towns and villages around — James Smith had a steadily growing business.

When James died in 1818 there was no question of his successful business closing down, and even when his son Charles Smith died so shortly afterwards, the business was kept going by trustees for his grandson Charles Winter to inherit when he came of age.

Charles Winter, a man of outstanding ability

Charles Winter, with shoemaking blood in his veins from both sides of the family, was a truly outstanding man. Not only did his remarkable energy and initiative create a flourishing shoe factory in Norwich employing 900 people but he also found the time to be a prominent figure in the civic affairs of Norwich.

Patrick Palgrave-Moore in his book, *The Mayors and Lord Mayors of Norwich, 1836—1974*, says that not only in business, but also in civic, social and political life Charles Winter displayed an extraordinary energy which earned him the admiration of all classes. He was a magistrate, and became sheriff in 1846 when J. J. Colman was mayor. He was himself mayor in 1851.

Charles Winter identified himself with the attempts to grapple with some of the stirring causes in the city arising from the rapid growth of population as people came in from the surrounding villages seeking work. Housing, sanitation and water supply were all woefully inadequate for the demands made on them.

He was, according to Palgrave-Moore, *persona grata* across party lines, being associated with such local worthies as Samuel Bignold of Norwich Union fame, Jacob Tillet, John Youngs, Robert Chamberlin and Henry Birkbeck.

Unfortunately there are no contemporary written records of Charles Winter's business achievements surviving, but the historians state that it took some years, probably until the 1840s or even later, before ready-made boots and shoes became a large industry, and made inroads into the dominance of the garret-masters.

The telling factor was the introduction of machinery in the factories on a scale that was impossible in houses. Winter is recognised as the first Norwich shoeman to use the sewing machine for closing uppers. Different dates are given, but that most diligent of researchers, W. L. Sparks, settles for 'about 1856'.

The next decade until Winter's death saw the introduction of more and more machinery for different operations, and a period of unprecedented growth, with the ready-mades selling both throughout the country and being exported to the Colonies.

To accommodate and provide materials for 900 workers, even if a large proportion of them still worked at home, and only came to the factory to pick up leather or partly made shoes, necessitated a large expansion of his grandfather's factory behind the shop. The premises extended by Winter

The St Peter's Street factory before it was demolished to make way for Norwich City Hall.

A painting by Sir Alfred Munnings to advertise the Lightfoot shoe.

SOFT AND GRACEFUL

FLEXFOOT

BEAUTIFUL FOOTWEAR FOR .. LADIES

Its remarkable Flexibility makes it the easiest of all Shoes and does not detract from its beauty and shapeliness

TENNIS SHOES
MANUFACTURED BY
James Southall & Co. Ltd. Norwich
:: FOUNDED 1792 ::

AWARDED DIPLOMA OF HONOUR

FRANCO-BRITISH EXHIBITION 1908

AS WORN BY THE LEADING TENNIS PLAYERS OF THE WORLD.

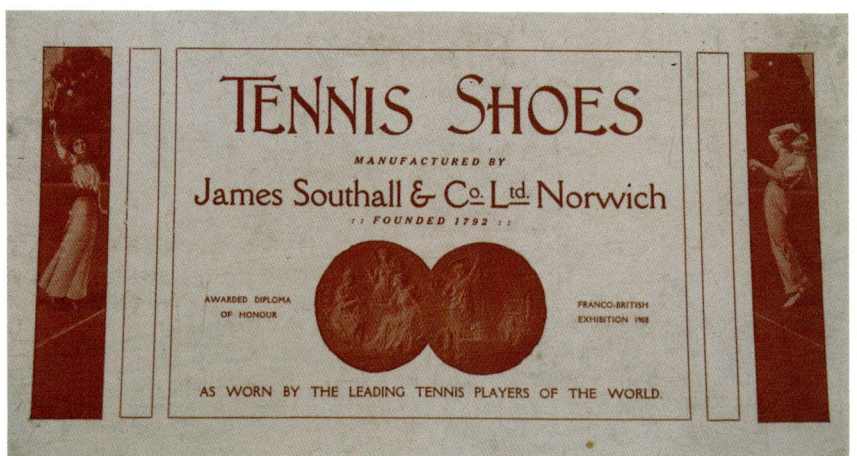

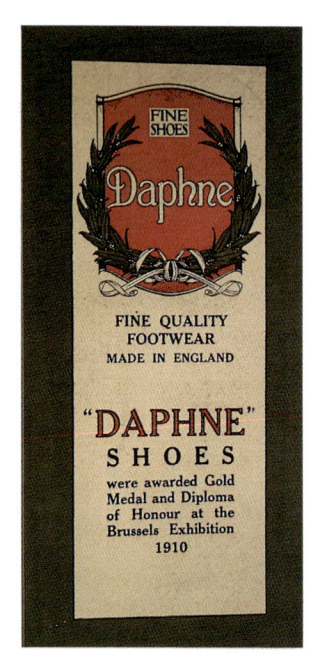

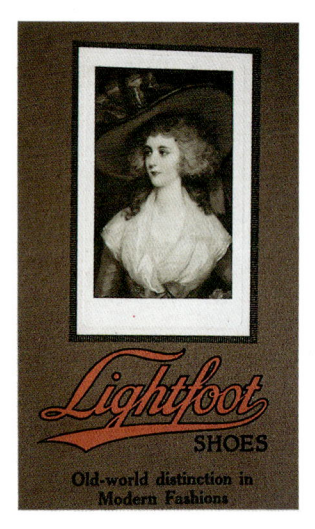

FINE SHOES

Daphne

FINE QUALITY FOOTWEAR
MADE IN ENGLAND

"DAPHNE" SHOES
were awarded Gold Medal and Diploma of Honour at the Brussels Exhibition 1910

Lightfoot
SHOES
Old-world distinction in Modern Fashions

Some of the showcards and advertisements for the fine and international prize-winning Southall shoes dating from the early days of this century.

For many years Southalls enjoyed wide renown as makers of top-quality ladies' fashion shoes. They won many awards at European shoe fairs such as this one at Turin in 1911.

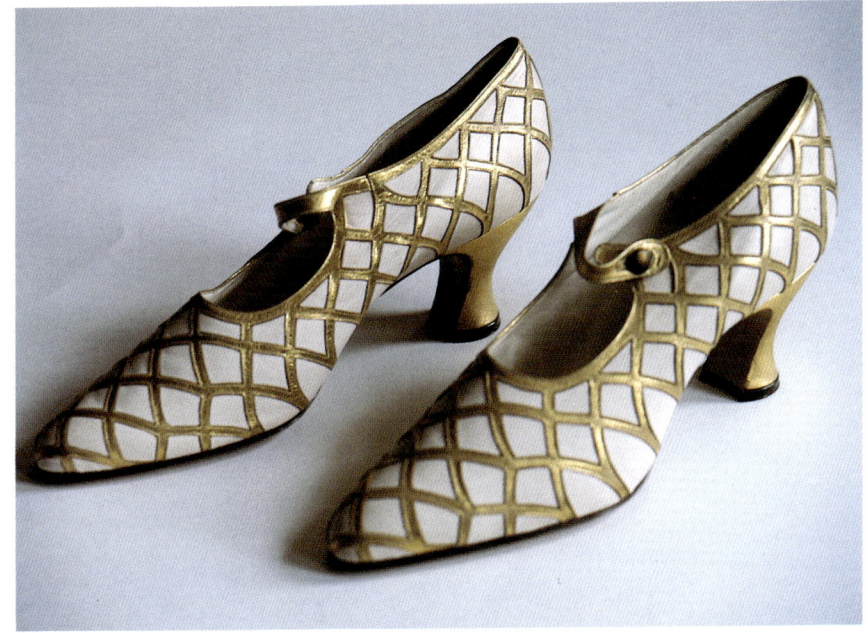

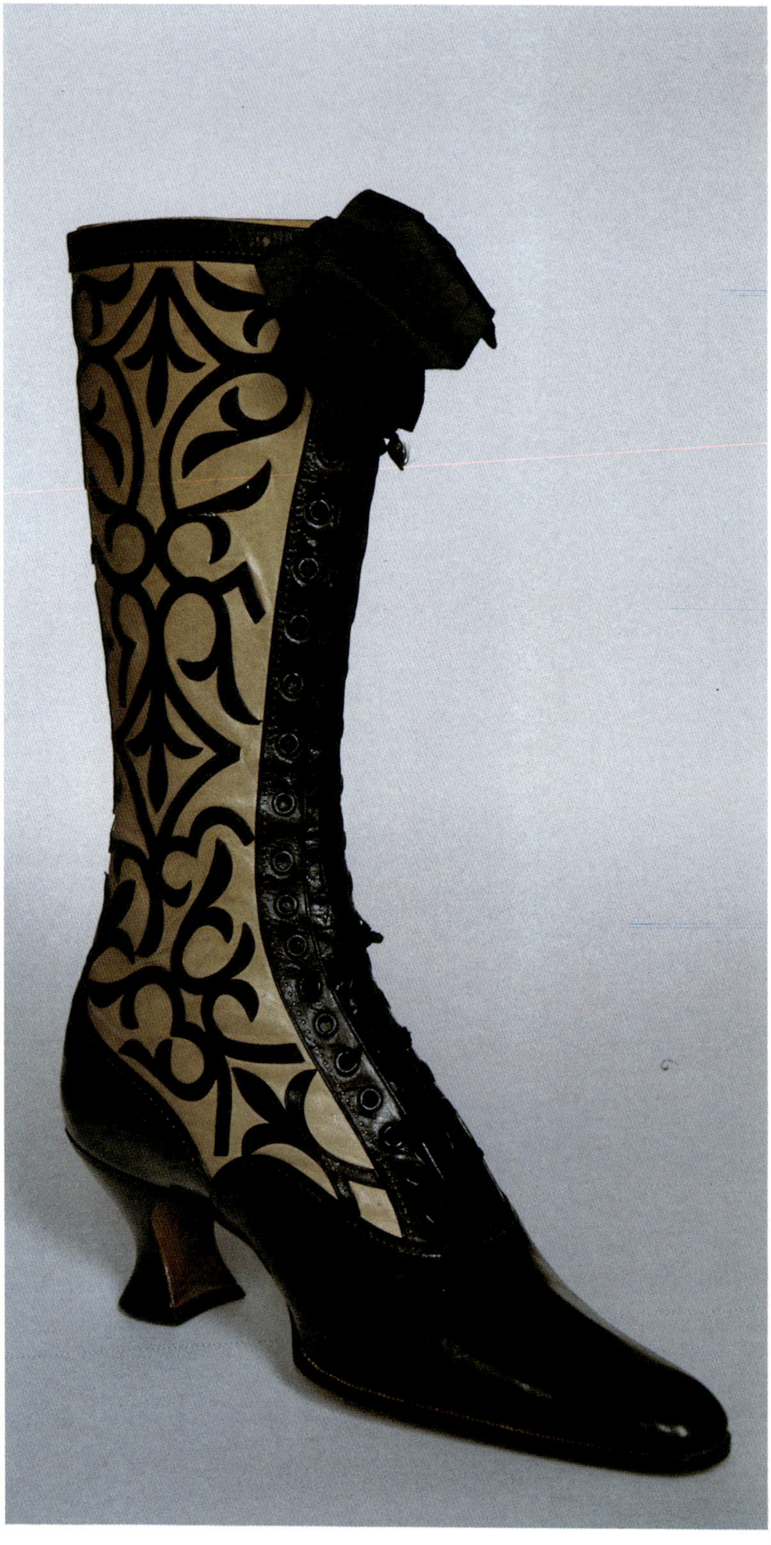
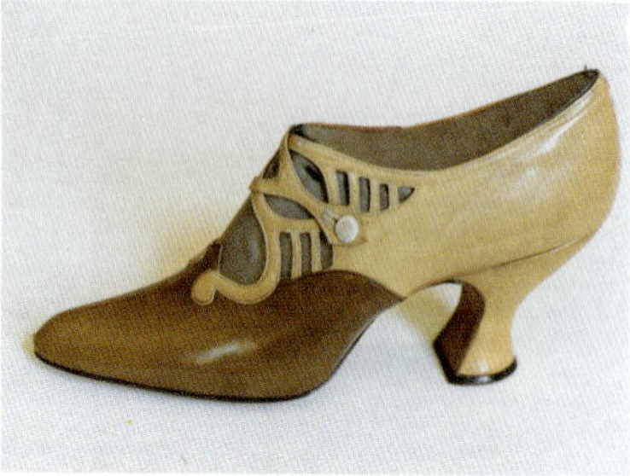
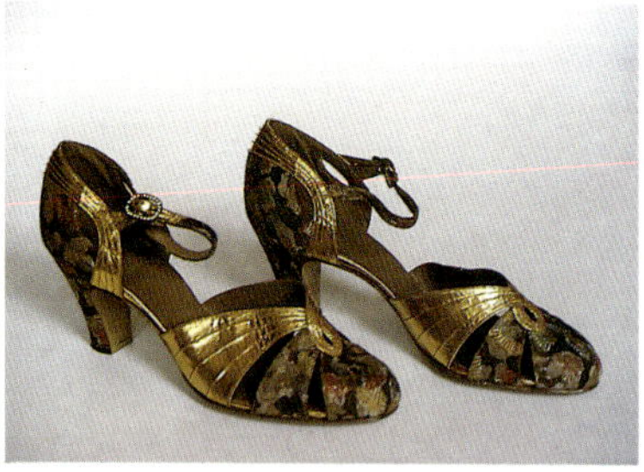
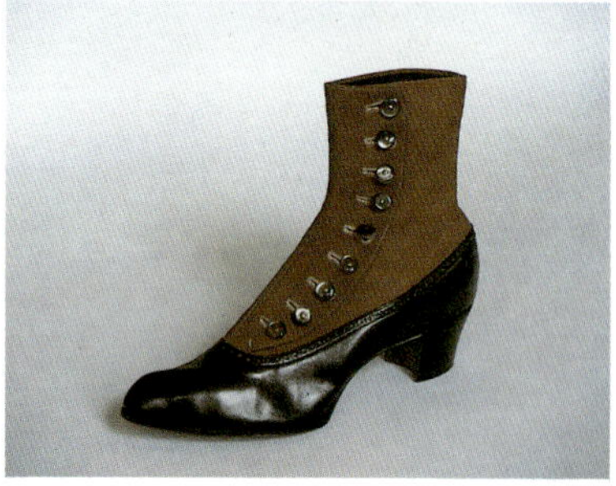
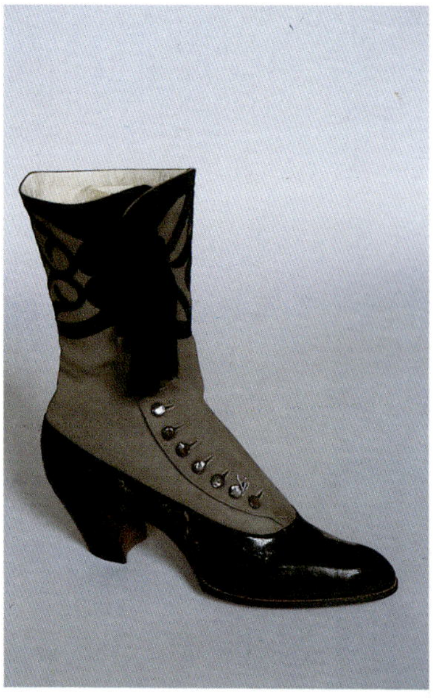

Few shoes survive for posterity to see. Among the few that the firm has from the many millions produced during its 200 years are some children's shoes and some of the dainty, elegant ladies' shoes and boots.

The ladies' shoes span the period from the late 1890s until the 1930s, many of them would be fashionable today.

from 1827 onwards must have stretched back towards the area now used as the City Hall car park.

There is a monument to Charles Winter's memory in St Peter Mancroft Church, Norwich. He died on 19 January 1867 at his residence in Heigham Grove, a house remembered for its unusual brickwork of a type not seen outside Norwich.

The partnership of Willis and Southall

Charles Winter's will, which ran to seventeen closely written pages, directed that the business should be offered for sale in whole or in part to his elder son, Charles Smith Winter. Sadly, he died only two months after his father.

Most of the money realised from the sale of the business was to be divided, in different degree, among his wife, his children and other members of the family, including the children of his deceased sister, Sarah Hannah. There were also charitable bequests to the Norfolk and Norwich Hospital, the Norwich Blind Institution and two local asylums.

It was the bequest to the children of his deceased sister Sarah Hannah which preserved the unbroken family link with England's oldest shoe manufacturing business. One of these children, Marianne Wells, had become the second wife of James Southall in 1857, marrying him at St Marylebone in London just over a year after the death of his first wife.

On his second marriage certificate James Southall is described as an accountant living at West Hackney, Middlesex, and the bride as the daughter of Edward Wells, a surgeon, living at St Marylebone. There can be little doubt that it was this family connection which brought James Southall to Norwich to work in Charles Winter's business in around 1860.

It is an assumption, but almost certainly correct, that his wife's inheritance left James Southall, the accountant, in the position to stake a claim in the future of the large and profitable Charles Winter business. He may have lacked a lifetime of shoemaking experience — although he must have gained considerable knowledge in seven years — but, even with his wife's inheritance, he is unlikely to have had sufficient capital to take on the large well-established firm employing hundreds of people alone.

Enter in 1868, John Willis, mentioned in the extremely scant records of nineteenth-century businesses surviving to this day, as a member of a Worcestershire shoemaking family. There was a firm of J. F. Willis in Worcester at the time making high-quality footwear under the brand name Cinderella. The factory is still standing.

There is also in the records a mention of a John Willis having come to Norwich from Gloucestershire. According to the 1861 Census the Willis family living at 375 High Street, Cheltenham, were shoemakers. The head of the family was John Willis, bootmaker, aged fifty-seven, who employed twelve men; his son, also John Willis, aged twenty-seven, is described as a shoe manufacturer employing thirty men and thirteen women. He must have been the Willis to travel eastwards to Norwich.

John Willis brought with him shoemaking experience and capital, for from the twenty years from 1868 until his death in 1888 his name took precedence. A catalogue of 1871 describes the firm as 'Willis & Southall (late Charles Winter)'.

Willis joined wholeheartedly into the life of Norwich, both socially and in civic affairs. He became a magistrate and an alderman, and it was through his advocacy that the Artisans' Dwellings Act was brought into force, and the deplorable dwellings known as The Rookeries in St Pauls were demolished to be replaced by the terraced houses still occupied today.

He also interested himself in the gas supply, and vigorously protested against what he held to be the unjust treatment of many people by the Gas Company, which he felt ought to be taken over by the Norwich Corporation. He refused the mayoralty because of failing health.

John Willis married in 1870 Mary Esther, the only sister of J. J. Colman of mustard fame, and lived at Southwell Lodge, Ipswich Road, Norwich, now part of the City College. His son, also John, was an academic, and did not enter the business, but he will be remembered by the older generation as a delightful personality who wrote engagingly about his world travels in the *Eastern Daily Press*, and left prodigious records and observations on the local weather.

John Willis's wife, born Esther Colman in 1838, as a member of one of the increasingly prosperous business families in Norwich at the time, must have been of benefit to the local business reputation of Willis & Southall. She was a remarkable woman, who lived until 1925. She could talk about driving to London by turnpike in a chaise with her father, and the beginnings of Colmans at Stoke near Norwich when a one-armed man did all the packing, except on busy days when she, as a tiny girl, would help him.

Willis & Southall 1871 catalogue.

James Southall takes over

With the death of John Willis at the comparatively early age of fifty-four, leaving teenaged children, the flourishing shoe manufacturing business of Willis & Southall passed into the sole control of James Southall, a name used to this day by older generations of Norwich people to describe the company equally as much as Start-rite.

James Southall, it is known, came to Norwich to join Charles Winter, his uncle by marriage, in 1860. He died in 1920 in his ninetieth year, and up to about a year before had remained firmly in control of the business as chairman of the limited liability company which was first registered on 24 May 1900.

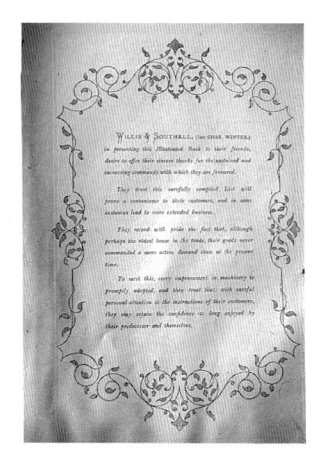

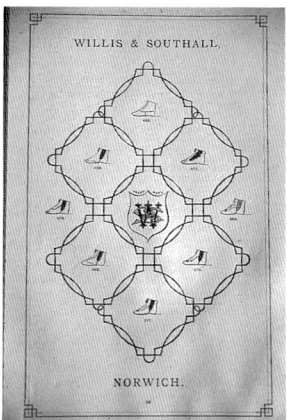

The company minutes of August 1919 record his absence through illness from the annual meeting of the company, the first one he had missed since it was formed. He was, however, back in the chair at the company meeting held very shortly before his death in February 1920.

Not a lot is known about the day-by-day affairs of the business during the latter part of the nineteenth century before it became a company, and was required by law to record decisions taken by directors at meetings. Even then the surviving leather-bound minute books in copper-plate handwriting contain summarised information, rather than a detailed account of the thinking behind the move from St Peter's Street to the new factory on the edge of George Borrow's Mousehold Heath.

Undoubtedly, Southalls continued as a powerful and prosperous business offering much-needed employment, and taking a prominent role in the establishment of Norwich as a centre for the manufacture of stylish, lightweight shoes for ladies, fashionable boots, evening shoes, and men's and women's slippers.

Much of the information we have comes from catalogues which have survived, and show that Southalls was making sandals and shoes for children during much of the nineteenth century, and as rail and sea communications improved the demand for British-made goods from the Colonies provided a soundly based and expanding export trade.

James Southall's sons, Charles and Frederick, born respectively in 1866 and 1874, joined the business, and became directors when the company was formed at the turn of the century with their father as chairman. But there is not the slightest doubt that James Southall was very much at the helm all his life, knew exactly what he wanted, and got it.

Hand-written minute books of the Southall company, signed by the chairman.

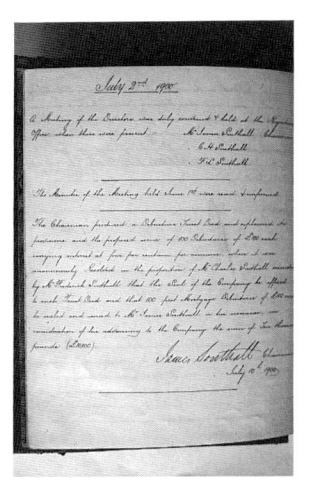

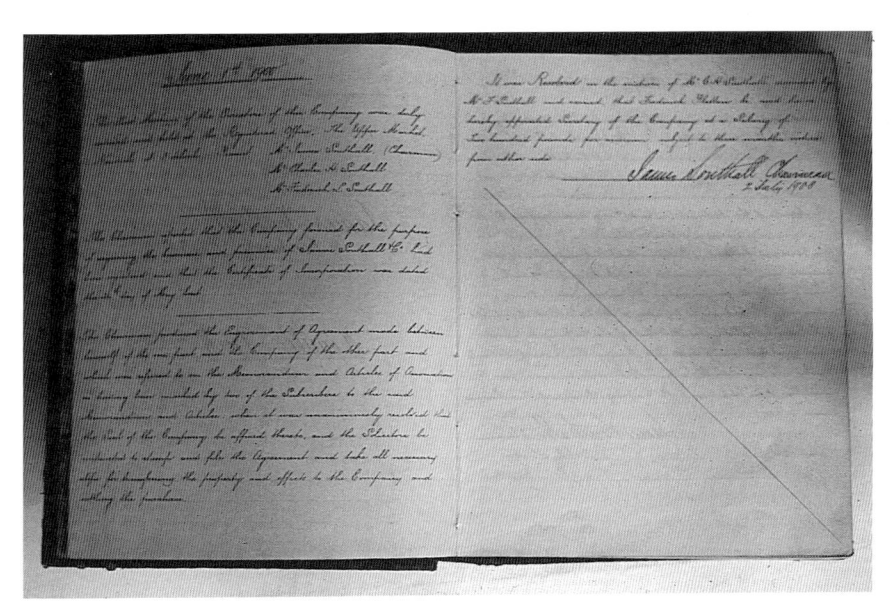

He was one of the prime movers in the formation of the Norwich Footwear Manufacturers' Association in 1891, and was its president right up to the time of his death. The introduction of shoemaking machinery into the factories by Charles Winter had been followed by others in Norwich as the numbers working in factories rather than at home continued to grow. And understandably, as the factories grew, labour disputes became common in a way which had been unknown with homeworking, where people either undertook to do an operation for an agreed price or did not accept the work. Those employed in the factories usually worked long hours for meagre rewards, even if they were better paid than in the declining local weaving trade.

The faults were not by any means all on the employers' side either. Many factory workers in the shoe trade found it hard to abandon the freedom of homeworking. They kept irregular hours, were undisciplined and unpredictable.

The manufacturers' organisation, and the operatives' union were already negotiating with one another in the shoemaking centre of Leicester in the mid 1870s, but even 120 years ago the *'du different'* syndrome was operative in Norwich. It was not until there was industrial trouble in 1890 that the Norwich manufacturers got together and formed their own association.

Twenty years before that, as machines began to take over in the factories, the boot and shoe workers began to organise. When, in 1873, no fewer than twenty-five workers from all over the country met in Stafford, one of them was from Norwich. They were mostly an uneasy alliance of hand-sewn shoe workers with a long craft tradition who were suspicious of the machine trade.

It was the Riveters and Finishers Union which was most amenable to trade union organisation when they took in the hand clickers. By 1890 the National Union of Boot and Shoe Operatives had taken over and was recruiting well even in Norwich.

An account of the formation of the Norwich Footwear Manufacturers' Association mentions the appointment of James Southall as first president — a position he held for the next thirty years. It includes a story, probably apocryphal, which none the less indicates the powerful decision-making ability of this man of business.

The story goes that the Association had only one meeting a year, and when it did meet the only item on the agenda was the re-election of the president. The first paid secretary, the late Herbert Gowen, a well-established Norwich accountant, liked to tell the story of how, soon after his appointment, he suggested to the president that it might be a good idea to hold quarterly meetings.

The great man eyed him from beneath his bushy brows, and said: 'You know the old saying Gowen, that a new broom sweeps clean?' The affirm-

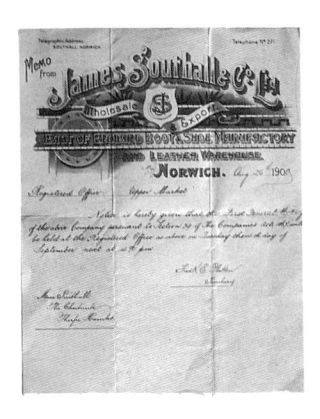

Notice of the first annual general meeting of the company.

ative answer was met with the response from James Southall, 'Well, we don't need any new brooms around here.' That was the end of any further thought of quarterly meetings...

This reminiscence comes from T. C. Jones who many years later, followed Mr Gowen as the Association secretary, and served the industry in Norwich very well. He was able to confirm that early records of the Association which would give an indication of the thinking of the founders were unlikely to exist and indeed may never have been written.

The same is true of written details of the Willis & Southall era, and also of Southalls until it became a limited liability company at the beginning of the twentieth century. The Victorian businessman's word was very much his bond, and his instructions were mainly given by word of mouth, with the heads of the companies very much in sole charge.

Even though they had formed a Norwich Association in 1891, it was not a member of any national federation. Most interesting among the limited number of old documents retained in the Start-rite archives was a uniform statement of wages of boot and shoe riveters and finishers for Norwich and district, agreed by the employers' and workmen's committee to come into operation on and after Saturday 26 July 1890. As well as setting out agreed wages for men, women, boys, and girls, the document set down the formation of a board of arbitration of six employers and six workmen. It was agreed to refer any dispute to the board without leaving work. It was signed by James Southall, chairman, BSMA and Benjamin Martin, honorary secretary, BSMA.

It is hard to know what else BSMA stood for if it was not the British Shoe Manufacturers' Association. Yet, in 1891, sixteen months later, the Federated Associations of Boot and Shoe Manufacturers of Great Britain held its first annual meeting at Leicester — and this was the much-respected organisation which celebrated its centenary in 1990.

It was towards the end of the 1914–18 war before the Norwich Association took part in Federation activities, showing that for the best part of thirty years, the Norwich manufacturers, led by James Southall, determined to go it alone, even though they recognised unions and believed in arbitration.

There was a long and expensive Norwich strike in 1897, aimed at compelling all the manufacturers to accept collective bargaining. It ended in failure, and cost the union £15,000, and a severe loss of influence, a situation which was not to be remedied for more than a decade. By this time membership had risen again and during the first decade of the twentieth century the Norwich shoe industry expanded, employing 10,000 people by 1910, with thousands of Norwich-made shoes being exported annually.

James Southall did not follow the example of his partner John Willis. He took little part in public affairs in Norwich. Following his death at his home, The Chestnuts, Carrow Road, the *Eastern Daily Press* of 6 February 1920

A wages book, dating from 1911, records amounts paid and earned which were seldom the same.

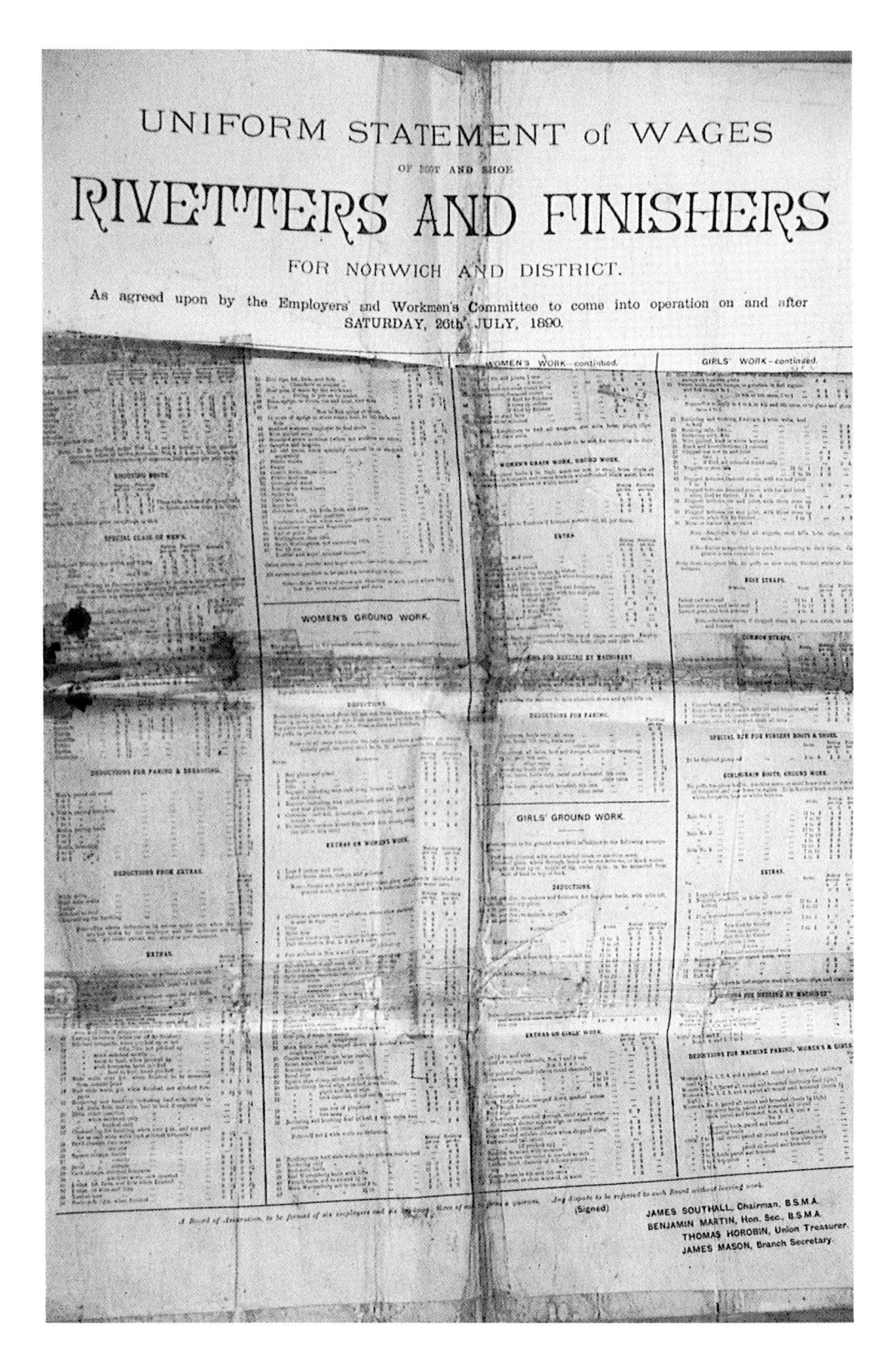

UNIFORM STATEMENT of WAGES
OF BOOT AND SHOE
RIVETTERS AND FINISHERS
FOR NORWICH AND DISTRICT.

As agreed upon by the Employers' and Workmen's Committee to come into operation on and after
SATURDAY, 26th JULY, 1890.

A poorly preserved historic document recording the agreement between Southalls and the Riveters and Finishers Union in 1890.

carried a long obituary which described him as a man of considerable resource, enterprise and untiring business application. It continued:

'He was scarcely less remarkable for a most retiring disposition, which was mainly responsible for his not entering enthusiastically into the public life of the city. Had he done so his counsels would have been invaluable.'

His one public interest, apart from charitable work, which included the presidency of the Boot and Shoe Trade Benevolent Institution, appears to have been the Norwich Omnibus Company, of which he was chairman for some time.

During the second half of the nineteenth century, leaders of the growing industries of Norwich must have been eager to see the development of public transport as the houses spread further and further away from the centre.

After plans drawn up in 1872 and 1878 came to nothing, the Norwich Omnibus Company began to operate in 1879 a group of horse-drawn bus services between Thorpe Station and Dereham Road, Newmarket Road via the Market Place to the Catton Whalebone, Unthank Road via the Market Place to Bracondale, and Earlham Road (College Road) via the Market Place to Thorpe Village.

The single-decker buses seated fourteen people inside, with another four or five people on top near the driver, and were pulled up the more steep inclines such as Guildhall Hill and near Thorpe Station with the additional help of a trace horse. The services continued until just before the Norwich Electric Tramways started in 1900.

James Southall was buried in the Rosary cemetery. The committal service was conducted by a Mr Primrose and a Mr Rice of the Plymouth Brethren, Haymarket Meeting at which he had worshipped, thus being a part of the Nonconformist and almost certainly Liberal tradition to which so many of the nineteenth-century business and industrial leaders belonged.

Export trade with the Colonies lost

When James Southall died in 1920 he was succeeded as company chairman by his son Frederick, who was then forty-six years old. Frederick's elder brother Charles, who had also become a director of the company at its inception in 1900, had died in 1909. The vacancy on the board had been filled by Bernard Hanly, who became James Southall's son-in-law in 1901 by marrying his daughter, Mabel Rosa.

As his father began to weaken occasionally as his ninetieth birthday approached, Frederick had deputised for him at meetings, and one cannot help but speculate that he must have found himself in the unaccustomed position of being able to take decisions for the first time without reference to the chairman.

The war years of 1914—18 were difficult ones for the Norwich shoe factories, with a loss of labour to the Armed Forces, a limitation of raw materials and a severe restriction of the export trade, which for some factories had amounted up to 40 per cent of their output.

There was no rationing of footwear, however, and manufacturers were able to sell all they could make. In addition, Norwich had large government orders on their books, for veldtschoen and machine-sewn hospital slippers by the thousand, which must have been the very thing for Southalls. The war, therefore, was not all bad for the shoe trade.

Just after the First World War, however, when Frederick Southall had become chairman, it was a different story. Much of the lost export trade could not be picked up again, as the overseas customers and Colonies had started to make their own boots and shoes. By the time the home market had been re-stocked in the early 1920s the trade was in a very depressed state.

At the first board meeting with Frederick Southall in the chair, in 1921, it was decided to reopen the factory on 17 January if orders permitted. This is the only reference to be found in the company minute books to the whole factory being closed, though seasonally, as is the custom of the trade, there had been short-time working in the various departments according to the production requirements and state of the orderbook.

There was a loss of £3,030 2s 7d (and 3 farthings) on the trading for the year ended April 1921, but with a balance of £24,454 the board decided to concentrate on marketing and selling their shoes. The new London

Girls taking part in a Lightfoot sales drive as early as 1913.

Start-rite's first staff representative in London, W. F. Bennett.

representative W. F. Bennett was provided with a car and a chauffeur, money was spent on advertising and all the representatives were instructed to do all they could to encourage retailers to buy in-stock shoes from Southalls.

This was also the time when the decision was made to place more emphasis on the new Start-rite brand, with Bernard Hanly, who had been a managing director since 1913, deputed by the board to appoint one person to be responsible for the production of the brand.

The fight back after the war proved successful. The shareholders received a 33 per cent dividend at the end of 1921–2, and the balance on the books had risen to £39,483. A home trade development committee was formed with the chairman Bernard Hanly, the company secretary F. G. Platten, G. W. Miles, W. F. Bennett, C. Walker and T. F. Southall on it. The committee was to meet every two months, with meetings limited to two hours' duration.

Frederick Southall, who was not blessed with the iron constitution of his father, saw the firm through the difficult years of post-war depression and price cutting in the shoe trade. By 1926 he had had enough, and he decided to retire. From then on he lived quietly at Thorpe until he died in June 1942 on the day before the death of his brother-in-law Bernard Hanly, who succeeded him as chairman of Southalls.

A tribute paid to his Uncle Frederick by James Hanly, recorded in the company minute books, indicates quite clearly that Frederick Southall's death was connected with the Baedeker air raids on Norwich in April 1942, but no further information could be found.

The firm gets a new Guv'nor

When Bernard Hanly was elected chairman at the company annual meeting in June 1927, it must have seemed to the office and factory staff at Crome Road that they had taken a step back in time. Those people today who still remember working under the new 'Guv'nor' recall him as equally decisive and single-minded as his father-in-law, James Southall had always been.

The Hanly family was of Irish extraction and had distinguished journalists among its members. One forebear, Michael Hanly, after taking his MA degree at Trinity College, Dublin, became one of the senior members of the Reporters' Gallery in the House of Commons, working for the *Morning Post*, and then *The Times*, for more than thirty years.

Members of the family were also involved with the *Colchester Chronicle*, and this is indeed where Bernard Hanly started working as a boy. It must be assumed, as others have done before and since, that he quickly discovered that the pleasures of a journalist's life did not always go hand-in-hand with unlimited prosperity.

Born in Colchester in 1872, he had worked for the *Colchester Chronicle* for eighteen months by 1887, and had decided that journalism was not for him. Even so, he appears to have made a good start, for the editor and proprietor of the *Colchester Chronicle* at the time, T. D. F. Micklethwaite, wrote to him:

Dear Bernard,

Nothing gives me greater pleasure than to bear testimony to your character and ability as I wish you every prosperity and success.

During the eighteen months you were on the staff of the *Colchester Chronicle* you were most attentive to your duties which you performed with every credit to yourself and your employer.

You had ample opportunity of acquiring a thorough knowledge of reporting, as well as the Publisher's department, and I was perfectly satisfied with you in both capacities. You have still youth on your side, and with a little more experience will be able to command a good position.

I always found you gentlemanly, and steady. With my best wishes for your future,

Yours faithfully

T. D. F. Micklethwaite

We next hear of Bernard Hanly as a young man learning about leather, and selling it, with a Northamptonshire company, which brought him to the different shoe centres, before he joined the office in the factory of S. A. Morgan, now the site of the Museum of Local Industry in the Bridewell, Norwich.

He joined Southalls in 1891, and set out to gain experience of the shoe industry in the areas beyond leather and office work where he already had some background. He worked on production in the factory under Charles Southall, and under the general oversight of James Southall, a man who expected to have all aspects of the business under his control.

Bernard Hanly, working closely with Charles Southall, made good progress not only with the firm, but also with the family as well, for in 1901 he became a member of it by marrying James Southall's youngest daughter, Mabel Rosa.

When Charles Southall died in 1909 at the early age of forty-three, only two years after the move to the new factory at Crome Road, Bernard Hanly was firmly in charge of factory management, and was then appointed to the board. Circumspect as they are in their recording of decisions, the minutes of meetings fail to disguise the fact that after Frederick Southall became chairman on the death of his father in 1920, he and Bernard Hanly had a number of differences on company policy.

When Bernard Hanly became chairman in 1927, after the early retirement of Frederick Southall, the company once more had an energetic and strong-minded leader who was both chairman and managing director. In addition to leading the firm creditably through the difficult years between the wars, he also found time to take a leading part in the footwear manufacturing industry nationally.

As the shoe trade's National Federation president in 1940—41, Bernard Hanly is remembered as a strong supporter of the Boot, Shoe, and Allied Trades Research Association (now SATRA).

He was instrumental in encouraging the Government to continue the grants which had been made to the Research Association on certain conditions, which included the important one of matching every pound subscribed by the manufacturers. He worked hard to obtain financial support from the industry for research, but held the opinion that the general body of manufacturers were unaware of its importance.

New methods of shoe manufacture, he said, were bringing in new materials, and difficulties were being experienced in using these materials, creating a need for scientific knowledge to solve the problems. And Southalls, he said, had received great help from the Research Association.

He was president of the Norwich Footwear Manufacturers' Association, for many years chairman of the local Arbitration Board, and was a fellow of the National Institution of the Boot and Shoe Industry. He was a founder member of the Norwich branch of the Institution, attending the inaugural meeting in May 1930 with G. N. Barrett, A. E. Bayfield, J. Bowthorpe, A. F. Durrant, F. Gook, A. G. Mann, H. W. Morris, A. F. Neve, E. A. Parker, and G. E. White.

His first high-level contact with municipal affairs was his appointment as Sheriff of Norwich in 1932, although for many years previously he had been a member of the board of management of the Norfolk and Norwich Hospital, and was its chairman in 1939. After his term of office as Sheriff he sat on Norwich City Council for three years as a Liberal member for the Thorpe Ward.

Pressure of business caused his resignation. Three years later he was again nominated, this time for the Ber Street ward, but he withdrew because of the war-time party truce. The following year he was, as a distinguished citizen outside the council, invited to be Lord Mayor, 'doing great service to the community as chief citizen' said the local press. Bernard Hanly was, at the same time, the shoe trade manufacturers' national president, and heavily involved with the Government to keep the shoe industry going despite the war-time problems.

He was also a magistrate, president of the Norwich Chamber of Commerce and the Norwich Rotary Club. Yachting and bowls were his recreations when he found time for them, and older pensioners recall that the 'Guv'nor' was no mean performer on the bowling green.

The young man who started his life in the Norwich shoe industry at about the age of eighteen with S. A. Morgan, in what is now the Bridewell Museum, had made a distinguished contribution, not only to the footwear industry and to Southalls, but also to the city of his adoption.

During the time he was the shoe trade manufacturers' national president, and also lord mayor of Norwich, he must have been in failing health, for the obituary notice in the *Eastern Daily Press* recording his death on 13 June 1942 says that it took place after a long illness borne with courage.

James Laffan Hanly

James Laffan Hanly, who succeeded his father Bernard as chairman of James Southall & Company, had joined the company in January 1925 at the age of twenty as a management trainee. He had a thorough grounding in the production processes, was sent to a Northampton factory for six months to widen his experience and was also put 'on the road' to gain some idea of selling.

Following the distress and disappointment he suffered after the last-minute cancellation of his intended marriage, he was sent on a world tour by his father with instructions to appraise, and wherever possible enhance, the Southall export business.

James Hanly returned six months later from this trip with James Southall & Company the main interest of his life and it was to remain so until his death.

J. L. Hanly at the time when he was a most active company chairman.

His first step, soon after his return was the greatly daring one of asking his powerful father for a rise from his initial salary of £150 per annum. He was given a small increase, but first it had to be referred to his uncle, Fred Southall, who, as the biggest shareholder, kept a keen eye on all financial matters from his home at Thorpe.

The well-authenticated story, told by James Hanly himself, was that Uncle Frederick, so scrupulous in his avoidance of nepotism, asked Fred Jex, one of the leaders of the shoe trade union in Norwich, about the merits of his nephew.

Fred Jex was a remarkable man who had a profound influence on the life of Norwich for many years. He must also have been a discerning judge of business ability, because it later transpired that what he had told Fred Southall, and indeed may have continued to tell him for the next twenty years, ensured that his nephew was left with sufficient shares to carry on the business when Bernard Hanly and Fred Southall died one day after the other in 1942, creating a crisis of succession in the firm.

This beneficial and positive opinion of his ability from the left of the political spectrum did not make James Hanly a convert to Socialism. Unlike his forebears the new head of James Southall & Company was a strong Tory supporter, with the firm contributing to Conservative party funds, and his reports to shareholders at annual meetings from time to time containing vitriolic references to the follies of the successive Labour governments and the inconsistencies of leading Socialist politicians.

Overall, he was a kind, gentle, self-effacing man, with an impish sense of humour, which greatly endeared him to all those who came in contact with him. It is surprising, considering his dominant father, that also he turned out to be a sound businessman. His surviving contemporaries, who worked in the business at the same time as father and son, Bernard and James, say that he was given minimum authority and allowed very little independent decision-making during his father's lifetime.

Yet James Hanly's contribution to Start-rite was immense, and the position of the firm today must be traced back directly to the forward-looking steps he made during the Second World War at a time when the future of Britain as a whole, let alone a shoe company based in Norwich, was far from certain. The decision to concentrate on Start-rite, and to make quality, fitting shoes for children in multi-width fittings on entirely new lasts, was indeed a very bold step to be decided on in the middle of a war.

While James Hanly did not follow his father in standing for Norwich City Council, despite being requested to contest a seat, he gave many hours

James Hanly shows Princess Marina around the Crome Road factory.

to public service of different kinds, as well as making a significant contribution to the welfare of the shoe industry, both nationally and locally.

He was three times president of the Norwich Footwear Manufacturers' Association, and chairman of its important Board of Arbitration and Conciliation. He was president of the Norwich Chamber of Commerce from 1946 until 1949, and was associated with the Norwich City Special Constabulary for twenty-three years, and was its commandant until being appointed a magistrate in 1961. He received a commendation for his valorous work during the 1942 Norwich air raids, particularly for his efforts in evacuating the Norfolk and Norwich Hospital during the blitz.

It is, of course, as a sportsman that so many people outside the shoe trade will remember him. As a young man he was a keen footballer, playing for Norwich CEYMS, and he also took an interest in shoe trade golf, though it was not a game he liked playing as much as tennis. He was still taking part in near county standard men's fours at tennis in his seventies.

He was a director of Norwich City Football Club for twenty-three years, seven of them as chairman, becoming president in 1970. Many people will recall the great days of 1959 when the third division Canaries reached the FA Cup semi-final after innumerable drawn games. After the drawn games production in the factory shot up on Mondays while the workers tried to earn the money for tickets, and perhaps travel costs, for the replays.

During the Second World War James Hanly had been active in the affairs of the British Footwear Manufacturers' Federation on behalf of the Norwich and other manufacturers. It was in 1945, when he had been selected as one of the delegates of the British footwear industry trade delegation to the United States, that his ship was torpedoed outside Dover, and he was picked up by a minesweeper. He seldom talked about this terrifying experience, and many who knew him well in future years were unaware of it.

He was president of the National Federation in 1954—55, and always keen on publicity for the British shoe trade, masterminding the national footwear exhibitions, and fashion shows associated with shoes, in London, Harrogate and elsewhere for many years.

He could also tell a good story against himself. One of the best was when a large number of manufacturers, heartily sick of the domination of the women's fashion trade by court shoes with what were called winklepicker toes and stiletto heels, decided that they were on the way out.

To make the point for the media, James Hanly, as chairman of the Federation Exhibition Committee, dressed as a Victorian undertaker with mourning weeds from his top hat, solemnly buried a winklepicker shoe in the grounds of the Majestic Hotel at Harrogate where the autumn shoe exhibition had its headquarters. It made for a good story and picture, and the media was there in force.

The only trouble was that the orders for the winklepicker did not

Presentation to James Hanly by W. B. Royce, BFMF President 1969-70, on his retirement as chairman of the Federation's Exhibition Management Committee.

diminish that season. They were as much in demand as ever, and even if the retail buyers at Harrogate were tempted to modify their initial orders because of the Federation view, they still had to increase them later.

Without doubt James Hanly also inherited the journalistic abilities of his forebears. He left some delightful sketches of Federation meetings, full of wry comments and innuendos, and one extremely humorous piece about a trip to Southern Ireland in search of his reputedly titled Irish ancestors.

Those who spent hours in his company, perhaps on business journeys, recall his wit and humour, and the way he would explain why he had taken some of the business decisions which had turned out to be so right for the company. Unfortunately, those were not the days when portable tape recorders were much in evidence. Neither did he write down his own business experiences, so a great deal of interesting detail died with him in 1985.

Start-rite children's shoes

Patent

The name Start-rite first appears in the company minutes after the 1914–18 war. In 1921 it is recorded that R. C. Base was interviewed for appointment as 'organiser' of the brand, and a couple of months later Quant & Son of Bury St Edmunds sold Southalls the exclusive right to use this trademark for their children's shoes.

Making shoes for children was nothing new. Catalogues which have been preserved, dating back well into the nineteenth century, illustrate boots and shoes for boys and girls, which sold widely in Britain and all over the world.

It was from the 1920s, however, that the importance of making shoes for children on special lasts evolved. It was seen that there was a commercial advantage, as well as important medical justification, in making shoes on lasts which were shaped like children's feet, and not merely scaled-down versions of adults' shoes incorporating all the horrors of current fashion.

Medical people began to express concern about the damage being done to children's feet by ill-fitting footwear, causing lifelong problems of mobility and leading to a painful old age. Once the damage had been done there was surgical and remedial footwear in abundance, but it was Southalls who made the first practical contribution to the *prevention* of damage to the young foot and its soft, pliable bones.

In 1928 the first organised investigation of children's feet in schools was made on behalf of Start-rite. This was some years after the first range of shoes was designed specifically for children with straight inside edges and the heel with the longer inside edge.

The name Start-rite was not an original idea for the new brand of children's shoes marketed by Southalls in about 1921. The firm's designers had responded to the thinking of the time that it was orthopaedically beneficial to make a shoe with the heel extended on the inner side (the Thomas heel) and a support inside the boot or shoe for the arch or instep.

Earlier thinking had tended towards a shoe with a stiffener extending around the heel on the inner side towards the ball of the foot, and with a spring to support the arch of the foot.

Awareness of the importance of fitting shoes to children's feet, rather than forcing the easily injured foot of a child into scaled-down versions of adult shoes, was due to a large extent to forward-looking retailers.

The *Footwear Organiser*, in an illustrated two-page article in its May 1921 issue, stated that the great change which had taken place in the

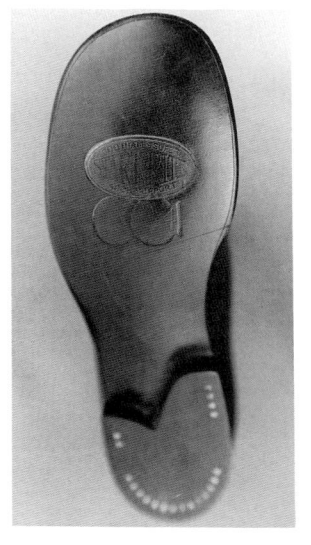

The Thomas heel, in use in 1921, but still used with the utility mark in the 1940s and with 'Southalls super arch support'.

attitude of parents was due to the enterprise of a few retailing firms. These firms had specialised in natureform footwear for children, and by catalogues, press announcements, and other forms of publicity, had brought about a revolution in attitudes to the fitting of children's footwear. The article said:

> 'In the whole realm of shoe retailing, nothing can give such personal satisfaction, or such sound business recompense, as the correct fitting of children's feet. When the child of today grows up he will bless the memory of the shoeman who took care of his feet when he was young.'

This article had been kept in the Southall archives, which like those of many a business concerned with current affairs, do not make the happiest of hunting grounds for the historian seeking a clear record of every significant happening in the company. The reason the *Footwear Organiser* of May 1921 had been kept was due, much more probably, to the fact that it also contained a report of Bernard Hanly's first speech as president of the Norwich Footwear Manufacturers' Association.

However, there is abundant evidence that in the very difficult trading times of the early 1920s there was an awareness at Southalls of the growing possibilities of the children's trade for fitting shoes allowing for growth of the young foot. Compared with the general run of children's shoes and boots, which had been made since the early days of the firm, this was a new and promising departure.

Nevertheless, it does seem that the *Footwear Organiser* was correct in suggesting that the stimulus for this potentially important market came from a small number of discerning retailers. One of those near Norwich, who must have influenced Southalls considerably was Quant & Son of Abbeygate, Bury St Edmunds.

It was Quant & Son who, to quote an indenture of 10 November 1921:

> 'have for some time past sold certain boots and shoes manufactured for them by James Southall & Company, which they have placed on the market under the registered trade designation or trade name of Start-rite.'

Under this indenture the partners in the Bury St Edmunds business, Percival Francis Quant, Percy James Bartholomew, Mark Stanley Petch and Hilda Florence Collison, granted Southalls throughout Great Britain and Ireland the use of the name Start-rite.

The consideration to the partners for the use of this name, which was to become world-renowned, was threepence for each dozen pairs of boots made and sold by Southalls under that name, or embodying the same salient points. The aggregate total cost of such royalties was not to exceed £500 in any one year — a wise precaution in view of sales figures over the years.

The agreement had a long and peaceful run, and after fifty years it was modified by mutual consent to the nominal sum of £100 per annum. This ceased on the death of Mr Petch, the last survivor of the original signatories.

The creation of the Start-rite company

Although the name Start-rite was first used in the factory more than seventy years ago, and gradually became a name to be reckoned with in the shoe trade, it was not until 1966 that the manufacturing and distribution company became Start-rite Shoes Ltd.

The suggestion that it would be wise to designate James Southall & Co. as the parent company, and create a new trading company, was made by the Norwich chartered accountant, David Gould.

He suggested that with James Southall & Co. as the parent company, the trading activities could be taken over by a different company. This would give many advantages, including tax savings.

The board quickly agreed, not only because of the financial benefit, but because, much more importantly, it allowed the new company to be called Start-rite Shoes Ltd, just at the time when that name had become much better known everywhere than Southall.

The nationwide survey

The decision of James Hanly in 1943 to review the whole basis of the Start-rite last was a bold one by the new young chairman and managing director. At that time there was an insatiable demand for all the children's shoes that could be produced with the labour and materials available.

The public counted themselves fortunate indeed to obtain a pair of well-made Start-rite children's shoes, and the retailers were on a strict quota. Obtaining usable leather and other components was a major preoccupation of management time; large-scale research was impossible, and there was a great temptation to be wholly concerned with current problems and not to look ahead.

Nevertheless, James Hanly decided on a nationwide enquiry into foot ailments and the scientific measurement of children's feet. He had the full backing of William Peake, originally a shoe designer who had a growing concern to produce shoes which fitted the many different sizes of children's feet correctly, and allowed them proper room for growth.

When these two men called on Harry Bradley, director of research of the British Boot, Shoe, and Allied Trades Research Association at Kettering, they found a kindred spirit who welcomed their suggestion of an

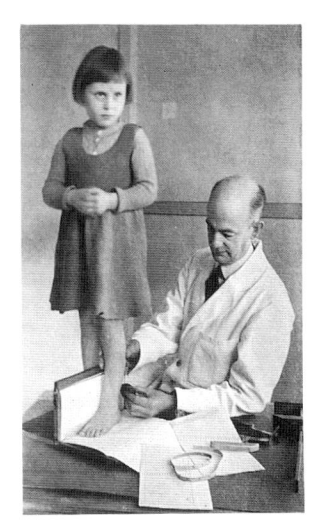

William Peake at work during the great survey of children's feet.

Seen here (second from right, next to James Hanly) is Dr Sayle Creer, the eminent orthopaedic specialist, who advised the company.

enquiry as widespread as possible at schools all over the country to obtain data to produce the most perfect series of lasts that could be determined by scientific use of statistics.

Without delay it was arranged that Mr Peake and Mr T. R. Garnet Lewis of the Research Association should conduct the great survey, beginning in Norwich in September of 1943.

It was found that both medical and educational authorities were most interested, and eager to co-operate. During the first week four schools were visited, and the feet of 106 children drawn and measured. The primary concern of the enquiry was not with surgical fitments — although foot deformities were being found depressingly frequently — but to produce the measurements which would allow production of a range of lasts which would cater as closely as possible for the natural shape of the child's foot, and allow for normal, unrestricted growth.

Nothing like the widespread war-time survey had ever been attempted before, and one of the early conclusions had to be that the existing Start-rite last, though good by the standards existing at the time, had been prepared on inadequate evidence. Divergences from earlier working statistics soon became apparent.

The statistics were recorded on a board on which the children stood evenly with a hinged leaf between their bare feet. A specially designed sheet of paper inserted under clips received tracings of the outlines, plantar and side elevations of both feet — six drawings in all. The name, age, sex, weight and height of the child were all recorded, along with vital foot measurements, and a note made of any special characteristics.

By the end of 1943, in war-time, with all its difficulties, more than 450 children's feet had been thoroughly checked, and the results tabulated. What became more evident was that it was impossible for any manufacturer to make lasts that would conform with medical opinion without some proper professional orthopaedic guidance.

It was here that an outstanding contribution was made by Dr Sayle Creer, an eminent orthopaedic specialist, practising in the Manchester area, who was most favourably impressed by Southalls' forward-looking view of their responsibilities to the nation's children. He took Mr Peake to two hospitals where he was visiting surgeon so that the Norwich shoeman could observe surgical aspects of their common concern.

This lead to Dr Sayle Creer becoming permanent orthopaedic adviser to Start-rite, opening up a new era in the manufacture of children's footwear, especially when his expertise was augmented by the co-operation back in Norwich of another distinguished orthopaedic surgeon, Mr G. K. McKee, later widely acknowledged for his pioneering work on replacement surgery. Just before his death last year Mr McKee recalled the pleasure he had had in working with William Peake in what he still regarded as an area of the utmost importance for a child's future mobility in adult life.

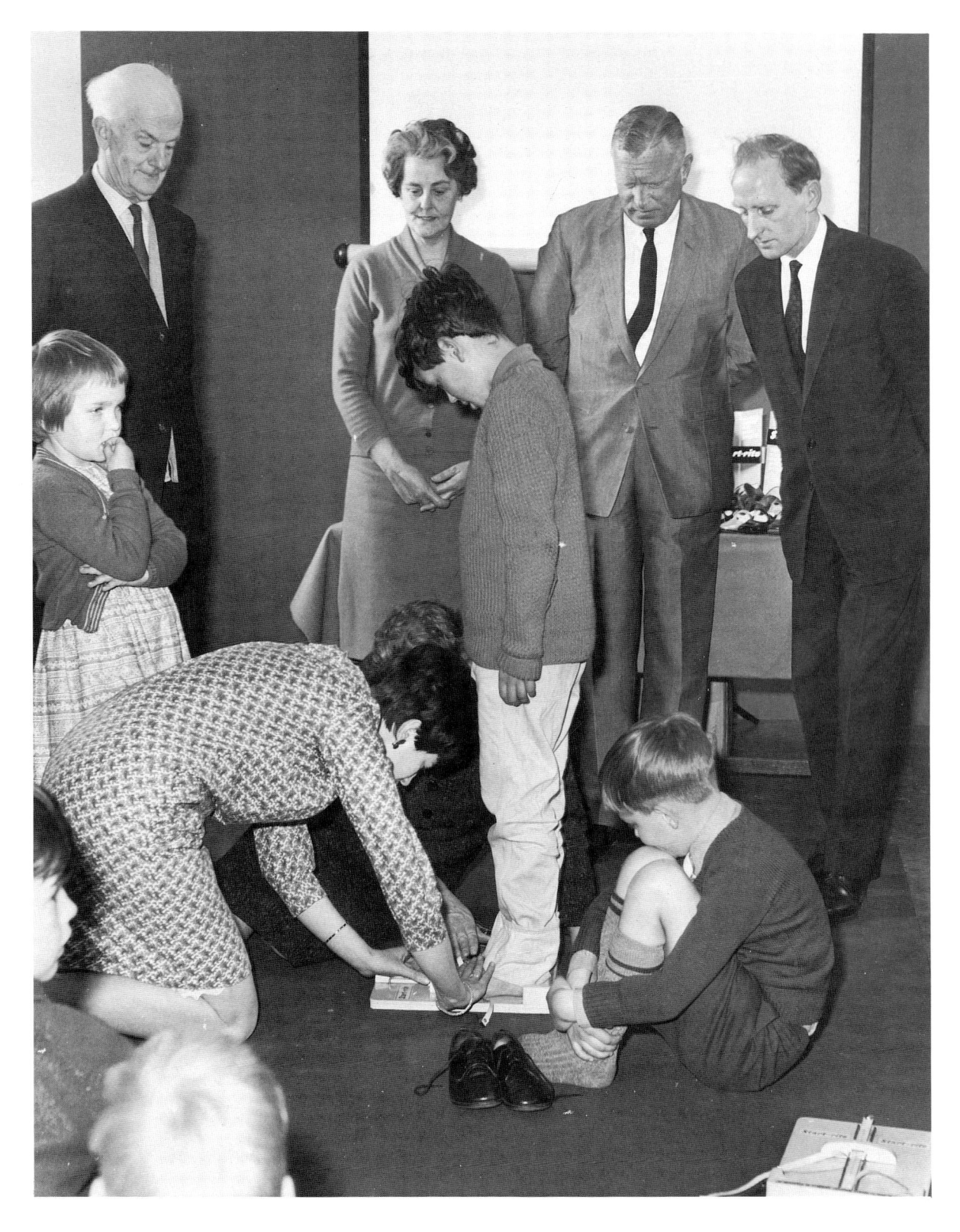

TWO CENTURIES OF SHOEMAKING: START-RITE 1792-1992

How the new Start-rite shoe differed

The Second World War had focused attention on the production of children's shoes as never before. The Board of Trade decreed that 85 per cent of the Southall output had to be children's shoes, which was a splendid opportunity for Start-rite when suitable materials were available.

The original Start-rite shoe in the early 1920s was an adaptation to large-scale factory production of a patented design known as the Thomas heel — an elongated heel on the inside of the shoe — and a specially constructed last.

The exhaustive checking of children's feet proved conclusively that what they needed was not merely an elongated heel, which, helpful as it was, had originally been designed as a remedial feature. The experts in the Norwich factory recognised that the real requirement for children right from the time they could walk, was for shoes which would encourage their tiny feet to grow properly without damage.

From then onwards the Start-rite last was widely recognised as the leader in children's fitting shoes. Sales took off in a big way to claim almost half the factory output in a remarkably short time. Southalls, as always, made very good quality shoes from the best materials available, and the updating of their manufacturing methods has continued to be a constant hallmark of the company during its two centuries in existence.

Stocked by agents throughout Britain, and with a range of 120 fittings, Start-rite had, by the outbreak of war in 1939, already become a household word, impressing itself on the consciousness not only of parents, but of medical authorities and educationalists.

James Hanly and William Peake realised that after the war there would be the opportunity to rekindle this immense amount of public goodwill and confidence in the name Start-rite. The thorough nationwide survey, new lasts approved by the medical authorities and ranges of well-designed fitting shoes in half sizes and width fittings was seen as the way ahead. How right they were.

Under the guidance of Dr Sayle Creer, and with the hard work of William Peake and his staff, the survey continued untiringly throughout the country during 1944 and into 1945 — north, south, east, west — with the different areas contributing to the mass of statistics collected.

Measurements had been taken, and diagnoses made, under official educational supervision, and with medical approval and assistance. Nothing had been left to chance, and no figures which could not stand up to expert examination were admitted to the final analysis.

The remaining problem was to turn the mass of statistics into a practical formula which would produce the shoes that were shown to be needed. As the survey progressed Mr Peake began to form a shrewd idea that the outstanding requirement for any new design was far more room — more

William Peake, Marjorie Bracey, James Hanly and 'Jimmy' James supervising a fitting session.

space for the toes, more width in the waist and more volume overall for the total space occupied by the foot within the shoe. Mr Peake wrote at the time:

> 'Formulae are not ends in themselves, the sole purpose of these minute and tireless measurings has been to help to produce a shoe which would encourage natural growth together with natural balance.'

Start-rite's concern had always been with prevention of damage to the growing foot so that children grew up healthy and mobile, without pain when taking part in any vigorous activity. But with the great survey showing up so many youngsters with serious defects the demand to make some form of remedial footwear for young feet that were inherently imperfect, or had been damaged by ill-fitting shoes, could not be ignored.

It was soon apparent that because the inner side of a child's foot ossifies later than the outside, it is prone to weakness unless the child's natural balance can be encouraged and maintained. In too many cases the child's foot rolls inwards to produce a permanent weakness, flat feet and other ills later in life. This was known as in-rolling or eversion.

Children's shoe manufacturers had found this problem difficult to deal with because a wedge added to the shoe did more to spoil the footwear than cure the foot, and could become acutely uncomfortable.

To deal with this the Inneraze shoe was developed having a built-in wedge as an integral part of its construction. Made of the then new plastic material, it could not be seen, could not wear, and could not be distorted or displaced.

Inneraze was the subject of an intense post-war advertising campaign and a film was made about its construction and benefits which was highly acclaimed by medical authorities in all the large centres of population where it was shown. Updated versions of the shoe still appear in the firm's catalogue, and continue to be in demand.

An early fitting course for retailers, 1947-48.

Senior fitting consultant Ron Reynolds, who has been instructing diploma students for nineteen years, explains the manufacture of shoes to a class of retailers from all parts of the country. Classes are now held in a purpose-built training school at Norwich.

A nationwide fitting service

Start-rite's long experience of quality shoemaking, design know-how and operative skills enabled them to make shoes for the growing foot that were unequalled. It was also recognised that it was pointless to make 120 different sizes of shoes, subtly graded to cope with growth forwards, sideways and upwards under the arch of the foot, if parents were simply going to buy them by size alone without proper fitting regularly and frequently.

From the time of the survey onwards fitting has been one of the basic features of the company, which regards the service given by those who sell its shoes to be as important as the shoes themselves. William Peake began fit-

START-RITE CHILDREN'S SHOES

ting courses for the principals of businesses selling the shoes and their assistants. From that day to this Start-rite shoes have been sold by trained fitters only.

The intensive course for shoefitters leads to the award of the Start-rite Diploma, the possession of which is regarded as essential for those who aim to progress in the area of selling children's shoes.

It must rate as more than a coincidence that William Chesworth, father of the present joint managing director of Start-rite, who was then a director of Lotus, attended the inaugural course. It was William Chesworth, who, when his son had completed his training in the Lotus factory, and sought wider experience, advised him to try for a job with Start-rite.

William Peake founded what has become a very important department of the company, training a thousand children's shoefitters every year, with diploma courses in the specially constructed Norwich training centre, in the regions, and by visits to stores and shops by the experienced and highly trained company fitting specialists.

Over the years there has been a constant feedback of information on the nature of children's feet, derived both from the fitting stool and from maintaining contact with schools and medical authorities.

The fitting services department, responsible for training retail staff, and liaison in the sales field, is regarded as one of the most important sections of the company.

William Peake, always a highly respected figure, and recalled by those still at Start-rite who remember him as 'a thorough gentleman', continued his outstanding leadership until he retired.

'Jimmy' James, who retired in 1990, congratulates his successor Charles Boyce, as head of the fitting services department.

START-RITE CHILDREN'S SHOES

Start-rite maintains its close connection with schools. Here (left to right) Gordon Harmer (production engineer), Mike Plunkett (designer), Ron Smith (senior pattern technician) and Charles Boyce (head of fitting services) test the 1992 styles on children's feet.

Charles James, always known as Jimmy, succeeded William Peake as head of the fitting services department in 1964, and for the next quarter of a century he was a zealous guardian of foot health, fitting and training those who sold Start-rite shoes. He retired in 1990, and was proud to receive a letter from the Royal Household thanking him for his services.

This responsible position is now filled by Charles Boyce, who had worked alongside Jimmy James for several years. His staff, strategically situated to cover the whole of Britain consists of Ronald Reynolds, Dennis Thorp and, to replace Jimmy James, a woman fitting consultant, Nancy Welland.

There are those who, because the soft young bones of infants' and even teenagers' feet can be damaged for life without any pain at the time by ill-fitting footwear, may say that the responsible manufacturers' constant reminders of this fact are so much hype, or deceptively inflated sales promotion.

These people would do well to read the 1973 Munro Report produced by a committee set up by the chancellor of the exchequer, and therefore completely independent of business pressures, which confirmed Start-rite's long-standing findings and led to a purchase tax exemption for young people's footwear.

By Royal Appointment

The seal of success on the development of Start-rite shoes, began in 1921, and carried on by James Hanly and William Peake, was the call to Buckingham Palace to fit the Royal children, culminating in the granting of the Royal Warrant by Queen Elizabeth in 1955.

This first-ever Royal Warrant granted to a Norwich shoe manufacturer was granted to James Southall & Co. who supplied shoes for the Duke of Cornwall and Princess Anne. It was, and remains, the only Royal Warrant in existence for supplying children's shoes.

The connection came about through the fact that Mr James Allan of Princes Street, Edinburgh, the head of a fine retail business now no longer in existence, had been going to Buckingham Palace, Windsor Castle, Holyroodhouse and Balmoral Castle to supply footwear to the Royal family for four generations.

Mr Allan had been supplying Start-rite shoes for the Royal children, and suggested that the supply and fitting should be properly taken over by the makers, especially as the children had worn Start-rites ever since they had been old enough to wear shoes.

Ever since then the Start-rite fitting services managers have been to the Royal palaces and houses fitting the ever-growing family of Royal children.

With all the Queen's children long since grown up, that Royal Warrant was withdrawn on 1 January 1989, and replaced by a new Royal Warrant of Appointment to Prince Charles from that date. David White described the continued Royal recognition of the quality of Start-rite shoes from one generation to the next as the best possible start to the New Year of 1989.

Prince Charles touring the factory during his visit at the start of the bi-centennial year.

Trade around the world

Exports

Since sole proprietors of businesses which they are working hard to build up would appear to have little time for the niceties of historical records, the precise area where James Smith sold his shoes is not known. It is unlikely, however, that he exported many shoes.

Neither do we know when Charles Winter extended his selling area beyond East Anglia, although the steady progress made right from the time the advantages of size standardisation were introduced by James Smith, meant that their footwear sold over an increasingly wide area.

By the 1860s when Norwich was connected to the deep sea ports by the railway, and agents were exporting all over the world in British ships, it is a safe assumption to make that shoes made by Winter's 800 to 900 workers were carried in some of the holds. Catalogues discovered a few years ago in a long-locked safe, dating from a little later in the nineteenth century, illustrate that the company carried on a flourishing trade for children's shoes both at home and overseas.

The earliest surviving catalogue dates from 1871, in the Willis & Southall era, but even here among the more than a thousand styles of women's and children's boots, and men's slippers illustrated, there is no direct reference to their availability overseas.

A large order leaves the loading dock in the early years at Crome Road.

In the company minutes of 1901 there is a self-congratulatory note about the success of business with South Africa, and within the next few years agents were appointed for South Africa, Australia and New Zealand, followed by Egypt, the Sudan, Spain, Portugal and the Canary Islands.

There is a record in 1902 of a South African firm obtaining registration of the then very well-known Southall trademark, Lightfoot, and the launching of the ultimately successful legal proceedings to reverse that decision.

It was only a few years later that Southalls began to exhibit at some of the leading overseas trade exhibitions, such as the Franco—British Exhibition in 1909, where the display of ladies' and children's boots and shoes won a diploma of honour. The following year space was taken at the Brussels Exhibition.

It was decided not to take part in the Utrecht International Fair in 1921, as 'the state of trade did not justify the expense'. However, the directors at that same meeting did manage to give £10 to Salvation Army Self Denial, an indication perhaps of the hardship around at a time when early in the New Year the board decided to reopen the factory on 17 January 'if orders permitted'.

Throughout the years up to the outbreak of the Second World War in 1939, Southalls continued to carry out their exports through the appointment of agents, who, if they were unsuccessful, seem to have been replaced quickly. It was something new when, in 1930, the chairman's son, the young James Hanly, was sent on a world tour which was said to have opened up some good export opportunities for the company.

Just before the end of the Second World War the company was active in checking up on the validity of its trademarks overseas, and James Hanly, who had by then succeeded his father Bernard as chairman, saw the United States and Canada as a potentially valuable market for children's shoes.

The new chairman visited the United States and Canada, and also South Africa where the agent, Mr Quick, wanted him to inspect a new factory and assess its suitability for the manufacture of pram shoes. Production began in South Africa, but as the firm was to discover more than once in the next few years, it was very difficult to achieve the same high home standards and make profits when manufacturing overseas.

Efforts continued to manufacture satisfactorily in South Africa with an investment in Romica Shoes (SA), but Romica Shoes went into liquidation. The firm's shareholding seemed to be worthless, but fortunately there appeared to be tax losses available for use by another South African company.

A firm named Jordan approached Start-rite to buy the Romica shares they held, and David White, then company secretary, was sent out to negotiate the sale. Jordan bought the shares and agreed to try to make Start-rite shoes, but again were unsuccessful.

It was but the continuation of a pattern which had existed since 1948, when Harry Jarmy, who was foreman of the stitchdown department at Crome Road went to the new Start-rite factory in Johannesburg, and helped to set it up ready for production.

He then joined the Mobbs Company at Port Elizabeth in 1950 when they undertook to make Start-rite shoes, and took over the assets of the defunct production unit at Johannesburg. He remained in charge of the Start-rite department there for some years, but found that the required output never rose above 400 pairs a day.

This, Harry Jarmy is convinced, was the main reason for the lack of success of the venture rather than any failure to maintain quality. There were relatively few white children to wear the shoes, and the great majority of the black children went barefoot. Harry continued to make casual shoes for Mobbs until he returned to work again at Crome Road in 1962.

During the post-war 'export or die' campaigns of the government, Southalls did their level best to earn overseas currency, and for some years they were remarkably successful. It was noted that in 1962 the growth of their overseas sales of Norwich-made shoes necessitated the company joining the Exports Guarantee Department of the Board of Trade. Later in that decade making children's shoes for export provided three months' work a year for the main factory.

In comparatively recent years the most rewarding overseas countries for Start-rite have been Canada, Australia and France. Australia picked up in a big way in the mid 1960s. Frank Martin, who worked in the import—export company William Sandover, in London, was initially responsible.

William Sandover's business in Australia was mainly in hardware, but a very good salesman in hardware, John Hardie, known to Frank Martin, was keen to have a go at selling Start-rite shoes. Then Alan Bennett, working closely with Frank Martin and John Hardie, set up a warehouse in Australia so that stockists could be given an adequate service. John Hardie was a great follower of the turf, and invariably timed his visits to England to review business to coincide with race meetings at Ascot!

The Australian venture prospered, and sales reached 100,000 pairs annually which was highly beneficial to the Start-rite factories, because the seasonal difference on the other side of the world meant that Australia wanted their shoes made at a time when pressure for supplies from home retailers was at its lowest.

After the political trauma created by the defeat of Prime Minister Gough Whitlam in 1975, prohibitive import duties and quotas made Australia one of the most protected markets in the developed world, but for many years from 1975 Start-rite's loyal customers, both consumer and retail, though smaller in number, were encouraged to continue their support of the brand. And, despite the substantial protectionist measures, the presence in the market was maintained.

Now, during the 1990s this protectionism is being eased, and Australia is expected to become, once again, one of the company's principal export markets.

It was very much the same success story in Canada, starting in the late 1960s. Inder Sharma was the successful agent backed by Start-rite, who worked from a well-stocked warehouse in Ottawa.

Directors and executives from Norwich were frequent visitors to Canada, and manned the stand at the Montreal Shoe Fair yearly, with the result that annual sales reached 80,000 pairs. However, after a decade or so of very satisfactory sales in the very important dollar market, quotas and high duties began to make exports to Canada impossible.

The great hopes of permanent success, indicated by a reference in the board minutes in March 1968 that exports were 40 per cent up on the previous year, were dashed by the imposition of quotas and tariffs not matched by any means on similar imports into Britain — an unhappy situation in the British shoe trade generally.

Start-rite shoes, however, made their mark in Canada, and journalists from that country who call at the Start-rite stand at the British shoe shows repeatedly ask when they will be back, without fully appreciating the problems of quotas and tariffs.

In his statement in the annual report at the end of 1968 the chairman James Hanly said that exports around the world had doubled in the previous two years, and the following year he was again able to report a 50 per cent increase in exports.

A notable contribution was also being made by Start-rite Shoes (Ireland) Ltd through the drive and initiative of Joe Cavanagh, the highly popular Irish agent, who was to be killed so tragically in a motor accident in 1985.

Shoes were made in Southern Ireland by Rawsons of Dundalk, and later by Laurel Shoes of Dundalk, but probably the most successful manufacturing venture in Eire was the cutting and closing of up to 4,000 pairs of uppers a week at Limerick. This proved to be a highly valuable contribution during the three-day week forced on British industry by the miners' strike early in 1974 when the Irish factory managed to send 5,600 pairs weekly to Norwich.

Sustained growth in France

With the virtual cessation of the Canadian and Australian markets for children's shoes from Britain because of prohibitive tariff and import quota restrictions, France has provided the Start-rite's best overseas market in recent years.

In 1958 Georges de Keghel of Brussels visited the Start-rite London office and made arrangements with Alan Bennett to sell Start-rite shoes in

TRADE AROUND THE WORLD

Start-rite in France. Advertising by one of the top French retailers.

Belgium, Luxembourg and France, and possibly, if he was travelling further afield, to visit customers in Germany, Switzerland and Austria.

He sold 700 pairs to a large firm in Austria, but the shoes did not sell well in Vienna, and there was no repeat order. Trials in Germany and the German part of Switzerland proved that the Start-rite shoes were not suited to the markets there either. However, at the Le Bourget Shoe Fair in the autumn of 1958, some trial orders were placed by Old England, Kent, Celine and Froment, all well-known Paris shops.

With these references Georges de Keghel made calls on other dealers, eventually selling to Till and Maralex, which became leading outlets for Start-rite children's shoes. Kent closed down, but Mrs Jolly, who had been responsible for sales there, opened her own shop, Cendrine, in Rue Vavin, Paris.

Year after year sales grew slowly, with Belgium doing better than France at first. The figures are interesting. During 1959, 400 pairs went to Belgium, and 80 for France; 1960, Belgium 4,400, France 1,000; 1961 Belgium 3,000, France 1,300; 1962, Belgium 2,300, France 900; 1963, Belgium 2,100, France 1,400.

From 1966 Belgium and France each bought about 3,000 pairs annually. Then in 1967 the French pairage doubled, and doubled again in 1968, reaching 13,000 pairs. Belgium remained at about 2,500 pairs because of increasing competition from Italy.

The French sales figure remained at between 12,000 to 13,000 pairs a year until 1974 when Bonpoint opened, and launched a traditional, black patent girls' shoe, followed by Till. Both advertised extensively, and it became highly successful. Eventually it reached French provincial towns where Till and Bonpoint opened branches.

Bonpoint introduced a great variety of colours into the shoes, and had some of their own designs made for them in Norwich. Till, with an increasing number of shops, became the biggest account, although Froment, with four shops in Paris, was still important. The Till and Bonpoint staff visited the Norwich factory late in the 1970s, which helped to increase sales, and in the 1980s some further members of the Till staff paid a visit to Norwich to mark the sale of the millionth pair of Start-rite shoes in France.

By 1980 there were about fifty shops in Paris and its suburbs selling Start-rite shoes and a hundred or so elsewhere in France, so that sales reached 77,000 pairs in 1984 when Georges de Keghel handed on to John Bennett, who resigned as export director of Start-rite, and became the company's French agent.

Georges de Keghel, who had also represented Church on the Continent, and had done a splendid job for the British shoe industry, was most deservedly awarded the MBE.

Into retail

Footwear manufacturers, particularly the branded houses, have always debated among themselves the wisdom of investing in retail outlets to sell the shoes they make.

Naturally, the temptation applies mainly to those who make shoes with a brand name that has been so well advertised it has become a household

The Start-rite shoes are some of the earlier ones of the brand and illustrate how today's fine shoes have developed from them. An ankle bar children's shoe made for the export market in the 1960s (top left). The S64 veldtschoen sandal which originated in the 1940s (above). The S37 machine-sewn one-bar shoe (top right). The highly popular S42 Oxford dating from 1950 (centre right). An ankle strap shoe with a glacé kid upper dating from the 1930s (below right).

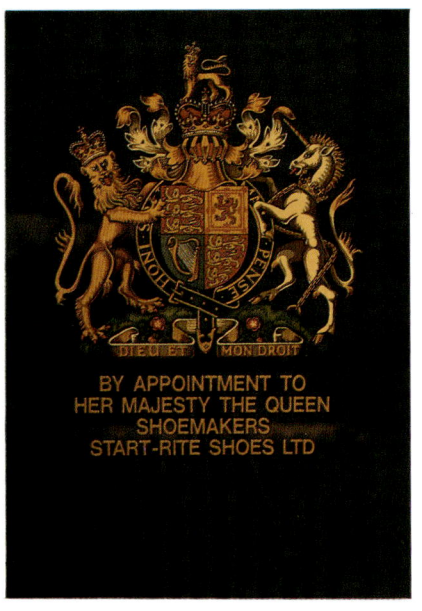

The Queen, Prince Philip, and the Prince and Princess of Wales photographed at Sandringham with Prince Harry, Peter Phillips, Zara Phillips and Prince William. All the children are wearing Start-rite shoes.

The two Royal Warrants.

The Start-rite twins have appeared in various guises and locations over the years, with different slogans.

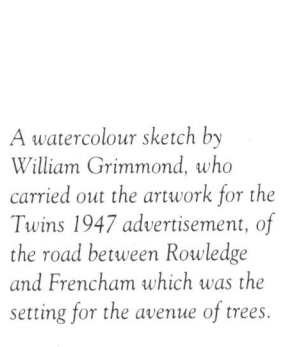

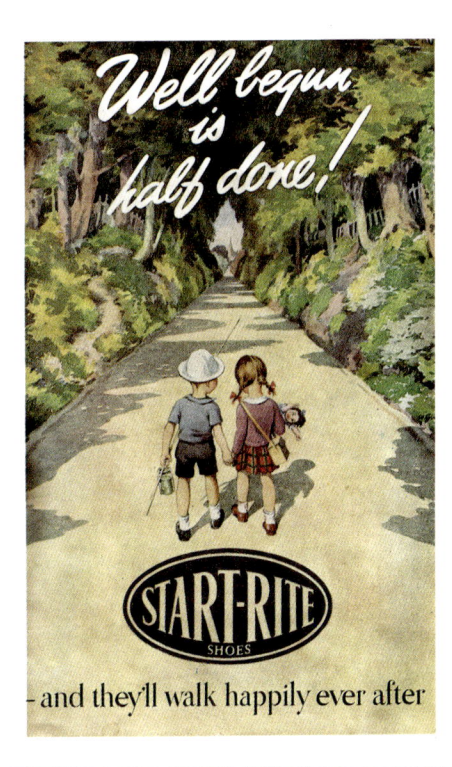

A watercolour sketch by William Grimmond, who carried out the artwork for the Twins 1947 advertisement, of the road between Rowledge and Frencham which was the setting for the avenue of trees.

Start-rite
shoes
TICKETS
Start-rite Special
Craftsman made in multiple fittings for good foot health

Start-rite
shoes have far to go
Craftsman made in multiple fittings for good foot health

The adventurous Twins have been by themselves on rail journeys and even to the moon.

word. Obviously, direct retailing by the manufacturer can upset other retailers who might find themselves in competition.

Furthermore, a retail arm which is not entirely independent can be persuaded to stock some of the manufacturer's less successful lines of shoes, which is a losing situation for both manufacturer and retailer.

Southalls had dropped the James Smith retail tradition but reconsidered entering the retail trade themselves in the 1930s at the behest, so it is remembered, of Fred Southall. Few manufacturers owned retail shops at this time, however, and the company decided not to do it.

Start-rite's first experience of retailing came about by accident through coming to the aid of customers who were in financial difficulties. It was in 1964 that Myers of Headingly, Leeds, had to be taken over to keep that good retail outlet for the Norwich firm in existence.

The shop sold men's, women's and children's shoes, providing the opportunity of an all-round experience of retailing. Under Start-rite management business was reasonably good, and a second shop was opened at Keighley. These shops were eventually sold to A. Jones.

The next venture into retailing was not until 1979 when John Bennett, grandson of W. F. Bennett, who had been appointed 'traveller for the London journey' in 1920, was given the board's backing to open a retail shop in Aylesbury with Hazel Cullimore. A second branch was opened in Cardiff and, as with Aylesbury, to help the business become established Start-rite stood guarantors.

It soon became apparent that the operation, and particularly the expansion of a retail company would require access to readily available capital and the benefit of management skilled in multiple footwear retailing. The two shops were taken into the Start-rite Group as the nucleus of what was to become Domani Retail.

The subsequent appointment of specialist management along with the imposition of a new retail policy and strategy has enabled those two initial outlets to develop into one of the most profitable multiple shoe retailers in the UK.

The point has been well proved that there is sound retail business in specialising in selling only children's footwear since the first children's-only shoe retail outlet was opened in the mid 1950s by Charlie Creswell in Chingford Mount, Essex. It was shortly after, in the late 1950s that Harry Fisher opened his children's-only shop in Hampstead Garden Suburb, selling Start-rite and Clarks shoes to become eventually one of Start-rite's largest outlets in the country.

It became apparent that the chosen name of First Footing was inclined to restrict sales to younger children. While this was a limiting factor it was not the main one for the disappointing financial returns overall. Some of the shops had been opened in expensive prime retail sites, such as the one at Wolverhampton. Experience showed that a good carefully selected retail site in a secondary or tertiary shopping area was much more financially viable particularly so if the area provided on-street car parking, or reasonably priced off-street car parking nearby. With a change of name from First Footing to Domani Retail, Start-rite's retail business became firmly established.

It has always been, and still remains, the company policy to open a Domani Retail outlet where the consumer demand for Start-rite products is not being satisfied and developed by existing stockists. The decline in recent years in the number of footwear retailers, both multiple and independent, has created the necessity for the company's own retail group to be expanded to ensure the availability of Start-rite nationwide, and eventually in Europe.

Now, in the bicentenary year, there are more than twenty-five Domani Retail outlets as the group pursues its policy of controlled expansion.

The retail business was given a substantial boost when in 1986 directors of Boots plc visited Start-rite to explain in confidence their plans for a series of 30,000 sq. ft. edge-of-town stores to be devoted entirely to children's products.

Start-rite was invited to run shoe departments in a number of these stores. The potential of this revolutionary idea was recognised at once by Start-rite, and the first department, with its distinctive decor and staff uniforms, was opened in Leicester in 1987, to be followed by several more in different parts of Britain.

Kennedys of Canterbury, founded in 1865, are probably the oldest retail customer of the Norwich firm, closely rivalled by W. J. French & Son of Southampton. Both have sold the Norwich-made shoes for a century or more. The photograph is of the Sun Street, Canterbury shop of Kennedys about 1900.

The growth of instock trading

Instock, the holding of vast quantities of shoes so that a retailer can replace quickly the shoes that he or she has sold, has become increasingly vital to the maker of branded shoes in recent years.

The word instock first appears in the Southall board minutes in 1920, and applied mostly to the Lightfoot and Thelma brands, with Start-rite coming increasingly into the scene, as advertising in the *Daily Mail* and *Daily Telegraph* in the mid 1920s created awareness of this quality children's shoe.

From the 1950s onwards much of the success of the firm's business has been due to mastering the intricacies of keeping the right shoes in stock in quantity, and ploughing the profits back into the business year after year to finance this undertaking.

Those who are nimble with their calculators may care to work out the impossibility for a retailer to stock even a large part of the Start-rite range in sizes, half-sizes, six widths and various colours.

Even with the retailer's selection of what he or she considers the customers are likely to find attractive, the stock requirement is such that a retailer must be in need of speedy replacement of lines in constant demand. The selection by the experts at the Norwich firm's headquarters of the shoes meriting repeat orders has become increasingly vital.

As sales increased it became more and more complicated to decide what shoes to hold in stock. Nobody can expect to get it right all the time, and the mid 1970s proved a very traumatic time.

Fashion was making an impact on the children's trade as never before, which did not help the sales of large stocks of traditional shoes. But even more significant in the longer term was the fall in the birth-rate. In 1964 there were 1,015,000 live births in Britain, and in 1975 only 696,000. So, the potential market had shrunk by one-third.

The fact that a growing number of the instock styles were no longer looked upon as fashionable by the target market could not be disregarded. A significantly large number of children would not wear the traditional shoes and sandals, and many schools were becoming less rigid about what their pupils were allowed to wear.

This change in demand resulted in over-stocking which had to be addressed. An automatic stock control system was developed which enabled both the retailers and Start-rite to control their stock levels through the company computer, the working of which, wrote James Hanly in an annual report to shareholders, 'is a secret shared only between the operator and the Almighty'.

It should be emphasised that not all the over-stocking was due to the impact of fashion; much of it could also be put down to the general trade recession when the shoe industry nationwide started to contract with the loss of over 4,000 jobs in 1975 alone.

Since then stock management has been a priority, with no effort spared to monitor closely the stock position in both manufacturing and for customers. The results of these efforts have been dramatic.

If in the 1960s and 1970s stock was turned twice in one year this was thought to be highly satisfactory. Start-rite now expect to turn stock six or seven times a year.

Staff outings of 1904 (top right) and 1930 (below right).

Employees remember

Ronnie Barker began in the Southall clicking department in 1930, and retired in 1981, but ten years later he was still working part-time on repairs in the rejects department. He has a remarkable memory of people and events about the company which is probably unrivalled and unrecorded.

He is sure, for instance, that the Lightfoot brand of ladies' shoes continued until 1953 when the making of ladies' shoes by Southalls ceased after more than 160 years.

He also remembers that, after the Second World War, former RAF buildings from Norfolk aerodromes, which were the only structures available without delay, were brought to Norwich and were erected at the back of the Crome Road factory to facilitate the production of big orders which the chairman James Hanly expected following a sales visit to the United States. The Nissen huts were to be used while obtaining planning permission for factory extensions. About this time the new canteen also opened.

There was great excitement at Crome Road at the potential of this post-war business with the wealthy United States, for although the company had shown firm intention of capturing the post-war quality children's shoe market in Britain it was still renowned for ladies' shoes.

The American business was to come through Mr Harold Florsheim, and the board minute books indicate that an agreement was drawn up but not signed. There was a lot of planning and negotiations with the Board of Trade to provide for the Florsheim production, and eventually it was agreed to go ahead, with production starting in March 1949.

Ronnie Barker continued the story:

> 'We cut hornback lizards, twenty pieces to every upper, and the clickers could only cut three or four an hour.
> 'We could not machine them, and they had to be sent down to Bristol. I remember that the samples were accepted by the Florsheim company, but the bulk was rejected.'

It was an unhappy experience for a firm approaching the end of making women's shoes after doing so for more than 150 years.

TRADE AROUND THE WORLD

TWO CENTURIES OF SHOEMAKING: START-RITE 1792-1992

The Angling and Gun Clubs of Southalls early in the century were well supported. The Gun Club, it is said, ceased in 1909, but the Angling Club appears to have flourished somewhat after then.

Between the wars, says Ronnie Barker, the factory output was between 9,000 and 11,000 pairs of shoes weekly, with a probable average of 10,000 pairs.

The first designer he remembers was Mr Harry Cox, followed by Mr Ayres who produced a court shoe with a pleated vamp which was unusual and won prizes. He also remembers Mr Ward as a designer, and then Billy Peake, who joined as a designer and then went on to carry out the great fitting survey and set up the fitting services department.

During the 1930s not many new styles were introduced in any one year. The favourites continued to be ordered in large numbers. Among those Ronnie Barker recalls which met with repeated success were Roughrider, a popular shoe for boys, but also worn by the more adventurous girls, and therefore an early unisex model. Roughrider was introduced in the second half of the 1950s.

Then there was Sunrider, a traditional sandal which had crêpe rubber soles. Louis Mills, the leather buyer, ordered 10,000 sq. ft. of leather every week for that style alone for about twenty years. From about 1930 until 1960 Albert and Grecian slippers, marketed under the name of Jascosie, were in almost constant production.

Apart from the use of crêpe for some sandals, all 1930s Start-rite shoes had leather soles and insoles which were all cut on the premises.

When he started work in 1930 Ronnie was paid 7s. weekly for a forty-eight-hour working week between 8am and 6pm, which was an improvement from the operatives' point of view on early in the century when the factory hours were until 7pm. His father started at the factory in 1909, aged twenty-three, at a wage of 14s. a week. When he married in 1910 his wages were increased to 17s. weekly. He retired in 1951.

Slow-time working was a fact of life in the clicking room during the 1930s, and of the ninety-two men employed there, it was customary for about twenty of them to be stood off at any one time. The foreman used to come with a worker's cards on the Friday evening and say that he would not be required again until he was called in. Boys were not stood off.

Asked to name some of the 'characters' of his long period at Crome Road, Ronnie first called to mind the managers and foremen. Charlie Base, who was in charge of production, would not be forgotten, also Mr Pointer, making room foreman, and Gillie Walker, foreman of the turnshoe room, 'Shady' Finch, the Reed brothers, Jimmy Neal, Billy Webb and Billy Abbs are some of the outstanding personalities whose names he recalls with pleasure.

Gillie Walker was a foreman of the stern mould. A retiring employee recently recalled his advice to any employee who was away sick frequently. 'You had better get a job to suit your complaint,' he would tell them.

There was always an emphasis on quality, and the Southalls reputation for making some of the finest light shoes in the world was a source of pride to

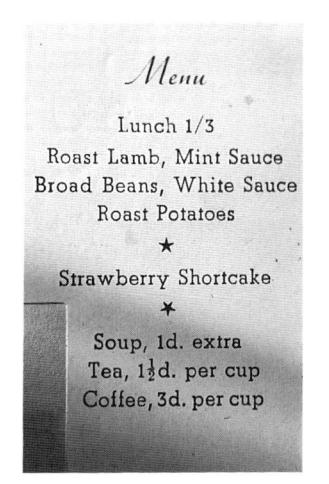

Menu

Lunch 1/3
Roast Lamb, Mint Sauce
Broad Beans, White Sauce
Roast Potatoes
★
Strawberry Shortcake
★
Soup, 1d. extra
Tea, 1½d. per cup
Coffee, 3d. per cup

Canteen meal for 6p! Late 1940s.

the operatives. Ronnie recalls Mr Sallows as the first person appointed specifically as quality manager, to be followed by Harry Ward and then Roger Hook.

Albert Durrant, who was clicking room foreman from 1923 to 1959, also taught the skills of clicking at Norwich Technical College three evenings a week. Miss Smith, Mrs Bussey, Lizzie Carver, Gertie Moore, Lily White, Gladys Plow and Winnie Ward were all well-remembered machine room supervisors.

Then there were Mr Pratt and Harry Pauling, finishing room foremen, Walter Lewin of the press room, Jimmy Smith of the preparation department, Billy Self and Claude Utting of the making room, and Mr Lambert the last maker. Ronnie Barker remembers working alongside members of the Smart, Palgrave, Oates, Barker and Richardson families, and others who had worked at Crome Road from the time it opened in 1907, and even before that at St Peter's Street, namely Reggie Abbott, Frank Barber, Harry Holman, Russell Beamish, Billy Freeman and Alfred Yeomans.

Sid Bannock of the dispatch department knew the names and addresses of all customers without looking at any book and Phyllis Bevan was one of the few women leather buyers in the whole industry. Never before or since, says Ronnie, has there been anyone so able at 'faking' or repairing a shoe fault than Lisa Parker, the trimming room forewoman.

Miss Marjorie Bracey started even earlier at Southalls than Ronnie Barker. She began in the offices in 1924, but finding the work there boring she transferred to the sample department. It was there that she first worked with Bernard Hanly, who kept a close eye on samples and costing, and later was chosen by him to run a special department dealing with special shoes for those with odd feet.

Princess Marina was one such customer, Miss Bracey recalls, because one of her feet was one-and-a-half sizes larger than the other one. Later, Miss Bracey became Bernard Hanly's secretary. She remembers him walking, hands behind his back, through the factory every morning. He would pick up shoes from the racks and examine them, with the foremen trying very hard not to be seen and questioned.

When James Hanly succeeded his father he had a very hard task, says Miss Bracey, because 'BJH' never really relinquished day-by-day control, even when he was president of the Manufacturers' Federation and lord mayor of Norwich at the same time.

Not only among the shareholders and executives of the firm, but also among employees too, there are families whose record of service goes back far into the nineteenth century. Long, continuous service both by men and women is the norm at Start-rite.

When the school-leaving age was fourteen it was a regular occurrence for a gold watch to be presented to employees to mark fifty years' service. A few watches were always kept in the safe. This continued until recently, for

Family service generation after generation has been a strong point with Start-rite. This is the Richardson family photographed in the later 1980s when no fewer than fifteen members of it were at work with 212 years of service between them.

in 1990 there were no fewer than four presentations for fifty years' service to men who had worked in the factory, and one to a woman retiring at the age of sixty with forty-five years' service. Minutes record earlier in the century the retirement of one employee with sixty-one years' continuous service.

Pensioners also seem to live on healthily for many years after retirement from Start-rite, such as eighty-eight-year-old Gertie Moore, who, when we spoke to her, was just leaving her bungalow to have a special hair-do for the Christmas party. Her father was a foreman in the heeling department and her brother, three nieces and a nephew had all worked for the company.

Finally, not from Ronnie Barker's memory this time, but from other sources, here is a tribute to the late Billy Abbs, one of the real Start-rite 'characters' he mentioned. He joined the company as a boy of fourteen, and retired in 1977 after working fifty-four years.

Known as 'Tiger' Abbs because of his ferocious tackling at half-back for the Start-rite football team, and because of his forthright attitude with colleagues, he played a cameo part in the single court case in which the company has been involved.

In 1976 a range of the senior girls' and boys' shoes failed in wear due to a faulty component.

The cost of returns from customers was growing so large that Start-rite sought compensation from the component supplier. The supplier denied liability, claiming poor quality control in the factory. Start-rite decided to take legal action.

It was a highly complicated case with a lot of technical evidence which took until June 1983 to reach the High Court in London and involved senior management — Roger Hook and Michael Chesworth in particular — in a great deal of work and anxiety.

The company was guided by Andrew Wood, a Norwich solicitor and

Even the pensioners are young and sprightly. Photographed in recent years at the Christmas party are Gertie Moore and Nelly Foldgate, both eighty-eight, Jim Aggas, ninety, and Russell Pinfold, eighty-one.

ably represented by Anthony Scrivener QC, later chairman of the Bar Council. As quality manager in 1976 Tiger Abbs was a key witness and he was brought out of retirement for the hearing in London.

The defending counsel made the mistake of trying to pressurise Tiger, who strongly defended himself in broadest Norfolk, more than once telling counsel that he was talking 'a load of old squit'. Also, he talked to the judge like a Dutch uncle, patiently explaining the intricacies of shoemaking and offering to make the judge a pair of glacé kid shoes — an offer which was politely declined.

After several days the case was settled out of court. When the long-drawn-out saga was over, Anthony Scrivener said that he had never dealt with clients who were more transparently honest — which must be rated among the nicest compliments ever paid to Start-rite or indeed any company.

A classic advertisement

The 'Start-rite Twins' posters and advertisements rank alongside the Bisto Kids, some of the famous Guinness successes and a few others, as some of the all-time greats.

The name Start-rite, as we know, originated soon after the First World War, but it was thirty years later when advertising and publicity about foot health, which so aptly keyed in with the name, really made it a household word. Eventually, it replaced the name Southall, and established the company as a leading manufacturer of shoes for the growing foot.

A letter written by James Hanly to the late Susan Beatrice Pearce RA in 1978 on her 100th birthday provides factual information of her involvement

TRADE AROUND THE WORLD

in the development of the famous advertisement. Mr Hanly wrote that he had been responsible for the production of the Start-rite Twins poster many years previously when the advertising agents had presented her very fine work of art.

'You may like to know', he wrote, 'that in addition to being featured in most of our advertising it has also formed the backcloth of a theatre production, Golden Pathway Annual, and that we sell a steady number of the 216-inch sheet posters, and mini-posters as well.'

In the mid 1930s, when he was working under his father, James Hanly advocated bigger expenditure on advertising, and indeed he discussed it with the London Press Exchange. The full effect of the move towards advertising more extensively at that time must have been curtailed by the Second World War. The much-admired Twins poster on the London Underground from 1947, showing them walking arm-in-arm up a tree-lined avenue, with the slogan 'Children's feet have far to go' made a tremendous impact, which, if anything, increased over the years.

With some slight modifications in the background and different slogans, the advertisement was widely used in posters, newspapers and magazines, and the Twins themselves were used as a logo, car stickers, badges, and in various other forms for many years.

A few years ago Miss Galpin of Wallingford, Oxfordshire, called at the Norwich offices to say that her mother Sylvia Galpin of Knowle Hill near Reading, and her uncle Gervase Craven of Hillingdon, Middlesex, had been the models for the Start-rite Twins.

Mrs Galpin and Mr Craven are twins, and it was their uncle, the late William Grimmond, who created the artwork for the London Underground advertisement in 1947. William Grimmond did artwork for the London Press Exchange advertising agency, and during the war had a studio at Rowledge, Surrey.

Mrs Galpin believes that the drawing was made in 1946, and her brother recalls the location as being a road near Bedales School. A picture of the scene was painted, and there was also a more stylised version with the avenue of trees. None of the original artwork sketches or paintings can be traced today.

It will not have escaped notice that the general 'feel' of the background of the celebrated poster owes more than a little to the illustration of the location in Kipling's *Just So Stories* trodden by 'The Cat Who Walked By Himself.'

For many years the Twins walking their never-ending road were seldom out of the public eye, and children often wrote in to say that their conduct was not in the best interests of road safety. The standard reply was that it was a private road in a park and so the Twins could safely walk up the middle of it.

When Start-rite decided to 'rest' the Twins in about 1970 there were a

The models for the famous 1947 advertisement on London Underground as they are today — Sylvia Galpin and her twin brother Gervase Craven.

TWO CENTURIES OF SHOEMAKING: START-RITE 1792-1992

The Twins advertisement as adapted by Tee Emm (opposite). (Above), the magazine cover and date, proving that the twins were known before 1947.

Joe Wilkinson, photographed in 1938 about the time he originated the Start-rite twins.

lot of complaints, and many letters to answer. They continued to create public interest, and a reference in the *Sunday Times* in 1980 to the origin of the classic advertisement in 1947 brought claims that it must in fact have been produced earlier.

Copies were produced of the RAF war-time magazine devised to promote safer flying, *Tee-Emm*, of Pilot Officer Prune fame, which regularly published drawings with the familiar national advertisements of the day adapted to make a point about air safety. The twins had been replaced by two pilots, an officer and a sergeant, walking up the familiar tree-lined avenue, with the slogans 'Pupil Pilots Have Much to Know', and 'Readers Learn Quickest and Fly Best'.

No records of the origins of this advertisement used before and during the war could be found, and inquiries were producing no response until Bill Wilkinson of Frinton-on-Sea was in touch with Start-rite on a business matter entirely unconnected with advertising, and happened to mention that his father, the late Joe Wilkinson had painted the twins' poster in 1938 for Stanley Studios of Sheffield where he was production manager at the time.

Joe Wilkinson's widow, Mrs W. L. Wilkinson, says that at that period Stanley Studios was a lively agency attracting work from all parts of the country, particularly advertising for the large amount of building development being carried out near London and in East Anglia at that time.

Her husband Joe was mainly a watercolour artist and, she says, was not particularly fond of, or good at, painting or drawing hands and faces, which is the reason for the back view, and the fact that the Twins are wearing mittens. The outline of the Twins has not been altered in any of the later versions.

Stanley Studios in Fargate, Sheffield, was blitzed in December 1940, and the probability is that all the artwork was lost. Sadly, none of the post-war artwork appears to have survived either.

While the twins must rate as the most successful of the company's advertising campaigns during its long history, there are other notable examples surviving, some of which we reproduce here. These include advertisements for the Southalls long-running and top-selling Lightfoot brand, at least one of which was the work of Alfred Munnings, later president of the Royal Academy, and distinguished painter of horses, who as a young man studied at Norwich Art School.

The home of Start-rite

Where it all began

We know that James Smith began his business in the Upper Market, or St Peter's Street, Norwich, in a shop with a warehouse or workshop behind it. It was successful, and under him, and his successors from Charles Winter onwards, it expanded to occupy the whole frontage between what was Wounded Hart Lane and Graham's Court.

The warehouse and workshop expanded backwards parallel with St Giles in the area close to that now occupied by the City Hall clock tower,

The frontage of St Peter's Street where James Smith had his shop. The Guildhall can be seen on the right of the picture.

Billy Mann, seated turnshoe-maker.

eventually becoming a very large factory right in the middle of the city.

A series of articles on prominent men in Norwich industry in about 1900, published by Edward Burgess & Sons of St Stephen's in 1903, and almost certainly written by Wilfred Burgess, a well-known Norwich journalist of the time, describes the factory in what must have been its heyday.

He gathered information about the firm from B. J. Hanly, then manufacturing manager, G. W. Miles, chief representative, and Frederick E. Platten, company secretary and chief accountant, and described the factory as he saw it. At the time the leather warehouse was entered from St Peter's Street, and by ascending a few stairs and turning to the right visitors reached the all-important counting house.

It was deemed worth commenting on that the warehouse full of superb high-grade footwear for ladies, brocaded and plain evening shoes, handmade goods, and children's shoes and sandals was contained in many thousands of boxes. Practically all the shoes made by the firm were boxed, which appears to have been something new at the time.

Wilfred Burgess then describes the works — the clicking room where 'scarcely a sound is heard', unlike the machine room where, under the supervision of Charles Mansfield, no fewer than twenty different machines were operated by the nimble fingers of girls and women.

There was also a visit to the press or punching room, which remained in use at St Peter's Street until well into the 1930s, while elsewhere, modified, but still working, one of the original Blake sole-stitching machines was to be seen.

One of the most interesting observations of historical interest was that in the turnshoe department almost all the men were standing at their work, but two or three of the older men found it impossible to adjust to this new method of working, and were seated. The older men could not earn a living wage if they had to work standing up, while the reverse was true for the younger men.

Finally, there was comment on the great success of Southalls' export trade to all parts of the world, which, together with the home trade, was maintained with 'scarcely unvarying success'. These must have been the halcyon days for this most cyclical of trades and this was surely the deciding factor in James Southall and his fellow directors deciding to build a new factory on what were then the city outskirts.

But before leaving St Peter's Street we should mention a delightful reminiscence told in the spring edition of the 1950 *Start-rite Footnotes* by Ernest Barber, director and company secretary, who had then been with the firm for fifty-four years.

As a lad in the front office in the late 1890s Ernest had plenty of time to watch people passing along St Peter's Street, and to listen to the cries from the fish market just around the corner. His main job was to pay outworkers when they brought in batches of work, amounts of money that frequently ended up in farthings.

Although farthings were frequently used in shopping and business transactions, there were not a lot of them about. So they had to be sought out and collected, not from the bank, but from the confectioner or greengrocer, or the stalls on the fishmarket which might even produce sixpennyworth of farthings covered in fish scales. Drapers, who sold lots of things with prices ending in the tempting elevenpence three-farthings, which was equivalent to today's sales price ending in ninety-nine pence, were never a profitable call. They needed the farthings themselves.

Bored young Ernest, with gaps between the outworkers calling for payments, found the sights and sounds of the streets outside a pleasant diversion. What better then than a note 'Gone after farthings' pinned on his desk flap as he nipped out into the market? Like all good things it came to an end. His frequent absences were noted and his quest for farthings had to be regulated.

As the use of machinery increased, and the mechanical processes produced a shoe-making operation without variation in the finished result, manufacturers seeking high standards and quality control used outworkers less and less. Ernest Barber's farthings were less in demand as ways and means of payment to reward skills which made the cost of the new machinery viable. The era of piecework was dawning.

When the present chairman, David White, started in 1957 in the costing office under Eddie Jones, who succeeded Ernest Barber, costings were still worked out to the nearest one-eighth of an old penny, and it was some years after decimalisation that the old money finally disappeared from costings calculations.

Shoemaking at Southalls in the past. Shoe room 1909 (top right), Turnshoe room around 1930 (below right).

The new Factory

Early in the twentieth century James Southall and his sons saw clearly that the way ahead for the production of shoes of a consistently high quality, and in a variety of different designs, on a large scale, was to have an up-to-date factory equipped with the latest machinery and providing good working conditions for the operatives.

There were obvious advantages in having the production area on one floor, and not at different levels in a multi-storey building as the older factories near the city centre tended to be.

A two-and-a-half acre river-front site off Barrack Street, now occupied by Jarrolds printing works, was considered, and other possible locations inspected before what was described as a two-acre site off the unadopted Silver Road was decided upon as the most suitable location for a new 25,000 sq. ft. shoe factory, offices and warehouse.

THE HOME OF START-RITE

TWO CENTURIES OF SHOEMAKING: START-RITE 1792-1992

Closing room late 1940s (top left) and Clicking room about 1930 (below left).

The architect selected was Ernest Buckingham, a member of a family of shoe retailers in Norwich, doubtless customers of Southalls. When Buckinghams celebrated their own centenary in the shoe trade in 1962, they brought out a delightful family publication, interesting for, among other things, a unique picture of one of the old home shoemakers walking through Elm Hill, Norwich, carrying about a dozen pairs of partly-made shoes strung on a pole. He was almost certainly on his way to the Bally factory which at that time was in Princes Street.

The architect's estimated cost for the building worked out at £2.9s per sq. ft., but it did not meet with the approval of James Southall and his fellow directors, who, during some months of 1906, carried out tough negotiations to bring the price down to £7,000. Eventually the contract was awarded to a Mr Self for £8,395, a £255 saving on the estimated price of £8,650 by the use of roof tiles rather than slates recommended by Mr Buckingham.

The directors then wisely decided to acquire or obtain on long lease additional land adjoining the new factory, the first acquisition recorded being in 1908 for an additional two-and-a-half acres behind the factory on a 999-year lease. There was no intention of giving up the factory in the city centre. Indeed, the decision to build at Crome Road was partly because of the impossibility of expanding sufficiently at St Peter's.

This was by no means the end of the alterations and extensions at both factories. Crome Road was considerably extended in 1909, further premises

An aerial picture of the Crome Road factory shows that externally little has changed since it was taken in the 1960s.

were hired at Wounded Hart Lane in 1919 and property was bought there the following year. Just before the First World War there was more building at Crome Road for more space in the stock room and shipping department. To this day there are constant changes, so that those now working at the CAD/CAM terminals may well be sitting where the turnshoe makers once stood or sat at their work.

It was during the depression in 1921 that the original factory began to be used less and less, the Norwich Corporation occupying the St Peter's finishing room as a vehicle store in 1921. Three years later the unsatisfactory state of the roof of the Crome Road factory was noted, suggesting that perhaps the economical use of tiles instead of slates had not been wise.

Modern times

The 1950s, a decade of change

The last forty-five years has been the most remarkable period during the 200-year history of the company. Start-rite has taken over, with the name conjuring up so many pleasant memories of childhood for so many people.

The directors were told at one of the first board meetings in 1945 that already Start-rite was going forward with increasing momentum, and there was every indication of a good future for the brand — a cautious understatement if ever there was one.

Plans were made to produce and stock the children's branded shoe to meet the sales that were expected from the publicity about fitting and foot health and the advertising in which James Hanly believed strongly, not to mention the efforts of a growing and increasingly professional sales team.

Quite quickly the brand necessitated more and more production space in the factory, and with the Southall shoes and slippers still being manufactured, there was a need for additional factory space and more women machinists. With war-time concentration to assist blitzed firms ending, the Roberts factory moving out and the opening of a small satellite factory at King's Lynn all helped. Women machinists were in great demand, with so many of those who had worked throughout the war becoming mothers now that their husbands were home.

The sales team, which had been depleted during the war, was back on the road, with shoes to sell, unlike the war-time quotas and a new London showroom was opened. This was at at 33 St George Street, bought for what today seems the astonishingly low price of £8,500. Many customers will still recall their visits to St George Street during the London Shoe Weeks, and calling at other times to do business there with Alan Bennett, who had succeeded his father, W. F. Bennett.

Start-rite sales continued to grow during the late 1940s, with every effort being made to get maximum production of the fitting quality children's shoes that the available labour, factory space at Norwich and King's Lynn, and machinery allowed. Good leather was at times hard to obtain.

Charles Base visited Leicester to see if the shoe factories there had ideas that would help with factory reorganisation to increase output. Experts came to Norwich to advise, and because of strict regulations on new building, where housing and war damage repairs took precedence, temporary buildings from former war-time Norfolk airfields were bought and erected behind the Crome Road factory.

TWO CENTURIES OF SHOEMAKING: START-RITE 1792-1992

No. 33 St George Street, the well-remembered former London headquarters, bought in the 1920s for £8,500.

The national fuel crises, and strikes by the nationalised industries all added to the problems of making enough shoes, but these were largely overcome by the installation of individual generators which provided sufficient power to keep the machines working.

By 1949 much of the factory building and reorganisation had been completed, and production rose to 16,000 pairs of shoes a week, or 800,000 a year, but still not enough to meet the growing demand for Start-rite. The product was right for the market, and with a constantly increasing child population as people obtained houses and settled down after the war, the prospects ahead were encouraging.

Southalls was still manufacturing women's shoes, but early in 1951 the board took a decision to increase the production of Start-rite and to make fewer shoes for women. This marked the phasing out of everything but children's shoes, finally achieved the following year. For children, less emphasis on the highly popular sandals was to be replaced by concentration on new styles of fitting high-quality back-to-school shoes approved by schools and education authorities.

It was not a change that was immediately successful, for there was a general trade depression in the High Street, resulting in some overstocking of shoes and short-time working in the factory.

Early in 1952 prices of Start-rite shoes were reduced in the hope of obtaining more orders and the board minutes recall the issue of warnings to sales staff not meeting their targets.

The 1952 results, with a net profit of £2,268 3s. 5d., showed 'nothing that gave any cause for satisfaction'. For Start-rite, however, this was the worst time, and although there is seldom a long period of uninterrupted prosperity in the footwear industry in Britain, prospects ahead for the Norwich firm began to show a steady improvement. Annual sales of the value of £1 million were in sight.

This landmark was achieved in 1954, when annual profits reached £23,628. The remaining years of the 1950s were a period of consolidation and progress, with the efficiency of stock control and sales analysis being improved by the introduction of Powers Samas — an early form of computers — and new scientific work systems being brought into the factory with union agreement.

The faith that James Hanly, Charles Base and others had in the future of Start-rite was soundly based. The company looked forward to a period of expansion with every confidence.

Start-rite bucks the industry's downward trend

Sadly, the contraction of the British shoe industry began in the late 1950s, continued in the 1960s, the 1970s and into the 1980s. Cheap foreign shoes, some at prices for which British manufacturers would be hard put to buy the materials, were being imported in greater quantities every year.

The low-priced shoes found ready buyers, and the retailers had to stock them. In the attempt to stay in business, many British manufacturers had to cut their prices, and therefore their quality standards, but still they could not compete.

Nationally, in 1955, UK manufacturers sold 169 million pairs of shoes to the home market, and sold 12 million abroad, employing 110,000 people. Only 9 per cent of the shoes sold in the shops were imported.

By 1989, however, UK manufacturers' sales had dropped to 114 million pairs, with 25 million exported. Sixty-seven per cent of the total of 266 million UK footwear sales was imported. The number employed in the industry had fallen to 47,000, well over 50 per cent down on 1955.

Norwich, with about thirty firms making shoes, and upwards of 10,000 workers in the industry in the years after the Second World War, has now only a handful of firms turning out footwear employing between them fewer than 2,000 people. Those firms which have survived are specialists in their particular field, the common survival factor being that they all produce high-quality shoes.

Start-rite, as the largest firm still in existence — with a payroll of around 800, as indeed it was in the mid nineteenth century — has had its problems from time to time, but it has managed to overcome them, usually very quickly, and achieve results out of step with many other manufacturers.

Once, when asked why Start-rite had continued to remain on a plateau when many other firms were depressed, James Hanly smiled and said that it was due to the children, whose feet, 'bless their little hearts', always grew.

But there has been much more to it than that over the years. A good product, finely produced and well marketed, with great attention to customers' needs, is partly the answer to 200 years in business.

Another vital factor, despite some temptations in the past, has been the resolute decision of the directors to keep the company as a private 'family' concern. The occasionally inevitable profitless year is accepted and understood by the shareholders. They are aware that they have become owners of a sound and successful company which has continued to finance itself over the years.

Also, a strong relationship with Barclays Bank going as far back as records of either companies go, along with a steady ploughing back of profits, has sustained the ongoing growth of Start-rite through two centuries of trading.

Unlike so many shoe manufacturers, who unfortunately had to close down as imports mounted, Start-rite was able to expand by taking over other Norwich footwear firms. The additional pairage was needed for several years when the company's problem was not how to sell its shoes, but how to manufacture enough shoes to pacify their customers.

The first acquisition made by Start-rite was in 1957 when the Ward Shoe Company was taken over. Wards was started in the early 1900s, and was bought by R. J. Howes in 1933. Its factory in Magdalen Street, Norwich had a reputation for making children's shoes of excellent quality.

Four years later the Bowhill & Hubbard business was purchased, and in 1966 that was the company that changed its name to Start-rite. In 1962 Start-rite Sonnet Holdings was launched, with 75 per cent of the shares being held by James Southall & Co. and the remainder divided between Kenneth Gooch and Eric Howlett. The Sonnet Company had been among the first in Britain to produce bright, colourful, eye-catching shoes for young children, instead of the usual blacks, browns and patents.

The Start-rite three-storey factory at Charing Cross, Norwich, where 100 operatives were employed, was completely burnt out one Saturday night in February 1964. Production was started three weeks later in adjoining premises using machinery brought from other Start-rite factories. As is typical of the friendship existing within the shoe manufacturing industry, the first company to telephone and offer help after the fire was one of the company's main competitors, Clarks of Street.

The whole issued share capital of R. Roberts (Norwich) Ltd was bought in 1974. R. Roberts was an experienced operative who had started on his own in 1926 making children's shoes. It is recorded that he produced them to sell wholesale at 2s. 11d. and at 3s. 11d. retail, with quality shoes at 3s. 4d. to sell at 4s. 6d. The business, which had been carried on at Crome Road during the war, was off Pottergate.

A further acquisition at this time was the Arthur Howlett factory founded in 1947 in Fishergate, and soon producing 3,000 pairs of children's shoes weekly. In 1968 it had become part of the Norvic Group, with Eric Howlett, who had worked for the British United Shoe Machinery Company in Australia, and was recognised as a skilful man on shoe production, remaining as managing director.

Still more production was needed, and many of the other shoe firms in the city were glad of the opportunity to keep their employees busy producing shoes for Start-rite. Negotiations started for a much larger factory at Page Stair Lane, King's Lynn and the large warehouse in Duke Street, Norwich, formerly occupied by Copemans, wholesale grocers, was leased to provide a larger and more efficient factory for Start-rite Sonnet.

Commenting on affairs during 1965 for his statement as chairman at the annual meeting in 1966, the chairman James Hanly was not by any means euphoric. He acknowledged a record sales figure, maintenance of profit level which would allow the same dividend and a splendid expansion of export trade with Start-rite selling in forty-six different countries.

The firm's 175th anniversary in 1967 reminded him of 1792, when the mobs were howling at the gates of the Palace of Versailles. Ever since then Southalls had traded successfully as a private company, but, he wondered, for how much longer? The Minister of Economic Affairs had said during a debate that the sooner private companies were put out of business the better. Mr Wilson's 'mob', he told shareholders, 'would have us to the guillotine'.

The boom years

Despite the chairman's frequent warnings to shareholders that in the prevailing economic conditions of the industry, and of Britain, they must not take satisfactory profits and dividends for granted, trade continued to be good for Start-rite in the mid and late 1960s.

The energetic efforts of the sales staff, who were instructed to call on customers frequently, and the experience of George Menzies as sales director, carefully watching over the instock department, kept the sales office busy.

George Menzies was a man with an outstanding personality and tremendous company to be with. Not only that, he was also a canny businessman with a superlative knowledge of the shoe trade. Although the title was never bestowed upon him he was, in effect, for many years joint managing director. Without doubt much of the Start-rite success in the late 1950s and the following decade was due to his drive and initiative.

In the 1960s the government-led export drive, and arduous overseas sales trips by directors and executives, had helped to double the firm's exports. As we have noted, sales overseas, particularly those in Canada and Australia, were providing three months' work every year in the Crome Road factory.

In 1969 the chairman's customary note of caution was not misplaced. The credit squeeze hit the footwear industry badly, and with cheaper imported footwear proving more and more attractive to the British people, some manufacturers found themselves in difficulties. For the first time in seventeen years Start-rite had not made more shoes than in the previous year.

However, a record turnover and increased profits was achieved once more in the following year, 1970, when David White was appointed joint managing director and Michael Chesworth joined the board as sales director on the retirement of George Menzies. These were to turn out to be the appointments of two men who would work well together in the years ahead.

David White, a nephew of James Hanly and grandson of Bernard Hanly, had taken a degree in history at Worcester College, Oxford, but deciding that it was not of sufficient practical use, later qualified as a chartered secretary.

George Menzies did an excellent job for Start-rite.

He joined Southalls to obtain the customary family grounding in the shoe industry, working mostly on the financial side of the business during his early years and gradually assuming wider responsibilities. He has a long association with the British Footwear Manufacturers' Association and the Norwich Association, following the family tradition of being a past president of both organisations.

His wide-ranging activities include service as a magistrate and fame as a witty after-dinner speaker, earned first of all not by speaking after dinner, but after lunch during the celebrations of the 150th anniversary of C.&J. Clark in 1975. James Hanly had nominated his nephew for this testing occasion for a young man, but he acquitted himself well. His witty speech, highlighting the fact that if 20 per cent inflation continued, then in one hundred years time shoes would cost millions of pounds sterling a pair, is still talked about.

Year after year the sales graph continued to move upwards, and other Norwich manufacturers of high-grade shoes were called upon to help, and were glad to do so. James Hanly, a cheerful, affable, though shy man, really had to work hard to include his customary note of caution when presenting shareholders with hugely successful results. Entry into the EEC in 1973 provided it. 'We may well find', he wrote, 'that we shall lose Commonwealth substance in chasing this Continental shadow.'

The total output of Start-rite branded shoes from all its factories, plus those bought-in from other Norwich firms, reached over two million a year by the early 1970s, and continued to increase. With approximately 1,400 employees Start-rite had become the biggest Norwich shoe manufacturer.

The director responsible for organising and controlling this feat of producing 50,000 shoes a week, with strict quality standards, in half-sizes and up to five width fittings, was Roger Hook, still production director and still with a good head of hair. He joined the company as a trainee in 1956, and three years later was quality manager. He was appointed production manager in 1961 and joined the board in 1964.

James Hanly was right. The children's feet did continue to grow, and with the large number of children born after the war themselves beginning to have families, there were lots of children needing shoes. Everything seemed set fair for Start-rite, but as every shoeman knows, trade in the industry never remains on a plateau; it has its ups and downs.

In the mid 1970s a combination of factors upset the climbing pattern of trade for the company. The enormous leap in oil prices caused a world trade recession; and as James Hanly had forecast, Commonwealth markets were lost by those countries imposing protective tariffs and import quotas; and developing countries emerged as major footwear producers. Fewer births had also reduced the potential home market by one-third.

At home the comprehensive schools which replaced the grammar schools were not insistent on school uniforms or selected patterns of footwear. The wearing of trainers imported from the developing countries abroad was also permitted for school as well as for leisure. Another significant thing was that even young children were demanding stylish shoes to reflect current fashion trends.

It was one thing to recognise the importance of fashion, as indeed the always excellent feedback from retailers had enabled Start-rite to do since the 1960s, but quite another to calculate its effect on sales. In 1970 the shareholders were told that if they looked in the windows of the shoe shops they would see that while the traditional virtues of good workmanship and good fitting had been preserved, a fashion element had been added to the shoes.

Later, and with understandable reluctance, was to follow recognition of the fact that the name of Start-rite, held with so much affection by many parents, and happily passed on to young children, could evoke resistance in some older children and especially teenagers. But, for the present, the matter requiring urgent attention and action was six different factories and a number of contractors working flat out to produce more shoes than were needed.

The parent company's turnover for 1974 had approached £6 million, having almost doubled in three years. At the end of 1975, in spite of cutbacks and some short-time working, the output of shoes was estimated to be running at an annual rate of 100,000 pairs above the likely sales figure.

With stocks rising both in Norwich and on retailers' shelves, cash-flow and budgets soon showed signs of considerable distress. The board of directors, with its young new members, knew that there was no current market for two million plus sales of Start-rite shoes a year, and action had to be taken.

Cut-back

Few people experience the strain involved by those responsible for the success of a large labour-intensive business. If it fails to make a profit it does not continue for long.

When all is going well, with workers and unions content, producing the right goods and selling them at a fair price just when they are wanted is rewarding and fulfilling for management. When, for economic and other reasons beyond control, sales plummet, necessitating production cuts and hardships for employees, it causes great anxiety and is emotionally draining for those at the top who have to take the decisions.

The position facing the Start-rite board in the mid 1970s was that there was a serious fall in the number of pairs of shoes being sold and it would be calamitous to go on producing them at the same rate, hoping that business would pick up. Also, it was becoming evident that technological change in shoemaking processes involving the use of computers, and other new techniques, were going to increase the pairage output of the operatives.

Once such processes are available in industry, a manufacturer has no alternative but to invest in them as soon as he can afford to do so, and is sure that they are right for his particular niche in the business. Failure to do so makes a firm commercially uncompetitive.

The brakes had to be put on sharply, causing a further shock to Norwich. Start-rite had become a phenomenon. Even those used to the ups and downs of the shoe industry had been lulled into a false sense of security by two decades of almost uninterrupted progress.

The first action was not to place further orders with other Norwich firms making shoes for Start-rite. Bally in 1974, and Sexton, Son & Everard in 1975 completed their last orders, followed by Trimfoot Shoes, a subsidiary of Shorten & Armes.

A bold three-decker headline in Norfolk's leading daily newspaper, the *Eastern Daily Press*, in February 1975, announcing that many of the 1,400 shoe operatives in Norwich making shoes for Start-rite would be going on a four-day week, was greeted almost with disbelief. This was something which had not happened for about twenty years.

Short-time working rather than immediate redundancy was tried initially in the hope that jobs could be saved and skilled labour retained for a future improvement in demand. But it soon became obvious that further measures had to be taken to reduce the number of employees beyond what could be achieved by not replacing those who retire or leave for other reasons.

At the end of 1975 the Start-rite Sonnet factory in Duke Street was closed and production transferred to the nearby Roberts factory. Fifty workers were transferred and seventeen were made redundant.

In May 1977 the decision was taken to close the Ward Shoe Company in Magdalen Street. About one-third of the 126 employees were found jobs in other Start-rite factories. It was a sad time for what had for so long been the city's staple industry, following as it did the closure of the formerly flourishing Sexton, Son & Everard factory, and the decision of the K Shoe Group to reduce its large shoemaking operation in Norwich to a closing room.

The appalling difficulties of the footwear industry continued, causing closures and amalgamations. There was over-production in the world footwear market, particularly at the cheaper end, depressing prices to the disadvantage of manufacturers. Pressure on governments, both Conservative and Labour, by the Manufacturers' Federation to obtain fair international trade and act against dumping of cheap imports had only limited success. It was, however, agreed to provide some financial assistance for reinvestment by the hard-hit industry.

Partly aided by a grant from this scheme, the modern 50,000 sq. ft. building which had been the former MacLaren handbag factory at

Mousehold Lane, Norwich was bought to become the firm's warehouse. The move made 20,000 sq. ft. of additional space available at Crome Road, enabling the Roberts factory and its 100 workers to be transferred there from Fishers Lane, and the Roberts freehold property was sold.

The final stage in what was a long-term plan for efficient and economic production was the necessary absorption in 1986 of the King's Lynn factory into the two production units remaining at Norwich. It was a decision which was economically necessary, but taken with extreme reluctance after the very useful contribution the West Norfolk unit had made for forty years.

New machinery and up-to-date technology enabled more and more shoes to be made in a smaller area, and with the additional space then available in the main factory, and the former Arthur Howlett factory in nearby Fishergate which had been purchased in 1973 remaining, there was ample space to make enough Start-rite shoes to fulfil realistic sales targets for the foreseeable future, with a limited amount of building land available if it became needed.

The young board takes over

This, as 1980 approached, was the beginning of a new era, with the young board of Start-rite Shoes of an average age of well below forty, intent on having a fresh look at every aspect of the way the firm was managed.

Although reduced in total, there was still a target market of thinking discerning people prepared to pay a little more for their children's shoes in order to have the benefits of research, manufacturing experience, proper fitting and high quality.

The new board of Start-rite Shoes consisted of David White as chairman, who had joined the firm in 1957, become a director in 1964, and was made joint managing director in 1970, and four other directors with considerable and varied experience in the shoe industry.

They were Roger Hook, production director, who had first joined the board in 1964, at the same time as David White; Michael Chesworth, director in charge of sales since 1970, who became responsible for marketing and development; and two new appointments, Michael Hull, with a responsibility for home sales and John Bennett in charge of exports.

John Bennett grandson of the company's first London salesman resigned in 1982 to set up his own import—export business in France, taking on from Georges de Keghel, and thus continuing his family's third-generation association with Southall and Start-rite.

The directors met much more frequently than had previously been thought necessary, and set about tackling the areas necessary for the survival of a specialist footwear manufacturing company in Britain at the time. It involved a long and detailed study.

Included were such things as a study of exports worldwide and a fresh look at the necessary fashion element in children's shoes, leading to the appointment of Harry Meekings as an experienced and highly regarded designer of fashion shoes. Job training, regular management briefings and, above all, Michael Chesworth's insistence that survival depended on top-quality shoes made from the best leathers and components, were among other subjects of prolonged discussion.

The pace of technological change in production methods was increasing all the time, and under the guidance of Roger Hook, choices had to be made from the bewildering number of extremely expensive alternatives on the right investments in plant and equipment to ensure the future of Start-rite.

The crisis in the firm's affairs caused by the inability to cut back production quickly enough to match the changing requirements of the market place had been overcome. Tight control on stocks and costs had brought back the situation where demand for shoes was slightly greater than the capacity to meet it. The going remained tough, however, with the number of good, independent retail outlets in prime selling positions in the city and town centres decreasing all the time.

By 1980 there was once more a chronic industrial recession affecting the purchasing power of the British people. The shoe industry was hard-hit, both nationally and locally, but Start-rite still managed to trade profitably.

Except for France, where the bilingual John Bennett was making a notable contribution to increased sales, the export market was depressing. Once more it was home sales — a rise in pairage of almost 10 per cent — which were the bedrock of the company's stability in an industry that was being decimated.

The achievement was all the more noteworthy because the overall market for British shoes in the UK continued to fall, so it represented a bigger share of available sales. It reflected great credit on the building of the range by Michael Chesworth and the efforts of the sales force, led by Michael Hull.

A further contribution to the success came from Roger Hook, production director, and his staff, who were managing to turn out an ever increasing number of high-quality shoes with reduced costs because of a much smaller factory area.

These factors all combined to boost trading profit for the Southall Group for the year ending in May 1982 to an 84 per cent increase over the previous year — a remarkable result considering the depressed state of much of the British footwear industry.

James Hanly struck the group chairman's predictably cautious note that in the overall circumstances such success could not be expected to continue. The following year, in his last annual review before his death in 1985, he was able to say that his warnings had, unfortunately, been fully justified. He was right in forecasting that the children's shoe business would remain extremely tough and competitive, but that Start-rite would continue to cope more successfully than most.

Periods of recession had become an inevitable and unavoidable factor in the UK economy, as with many other developed nations. The recession of the early 1980s, heightened by a campaign of consumerism, generated by the media, with footwear a particular target, made 1984 an extremely difficult year. The response was quicker, but in ten years trading patterns had changed so dramatically that the problems were deeper. Trading results took an alarming downturn, and the firm faced only its second recorded loss since records were established.

Production was once again restrained, and in-depth reviews of quality control systems, retail operations and development programmes were initiated.

Quality, forever at the core of Start-rite products, was to be even more a key element in the firm's current and future marketing strategy. Through investment, management would be unsparing in its efforts to achieve ever higher standards.

The retail trade, badly hit by the recession, presented a consumer market in decline, and the Start-rite retail group had not been spared. Although this time the effects of the recession were felt more sharply in the North and in Scotland, a ripple effect still permeated through all areas.

The changing demands of the consumer now meant the creation of some forty new styles each season. These styles not only had to look attractive through their design, but had to be engineered to ensure a trouble-free cost-effective flow through the production process. There was no quick, inexpensive way of achieving this.

Intensive pressures as experienced in the 1970s had to be faced once more, but it was rightly felt that the team which had previously shown itself capable of producing good results was the one to take on this new challenge. In many ways the lossmaking year of 1984 provided a better education than all the good years.

From the review of all company operations changes were dictated in many areas. A planned strengthening of management to enable the introduction of new technology and systems to enhance profits, service and product development was begun.

Hard lessons were also well learned in the retail operation. Those units shown as unable to achieve the level of profitability required were scheduled for closure, and long-term plans for the development of new units and management put into place.

The general review of the company's operations had the desired effect. Profit share was introduced as a key element in the greater involvement of management in the company's future. Remarkably quickly, the loss of 1984 was turned into a modest profit in 1985, allowing thoughts to return once

Making a Start-rite or Domani shoe for 1992.

(i) Harry Meekings (left) and his design team deciding on the styles.

(ii) Maurice Rudd (left) and Terry Norman (right) selecting the upper leather from a stock valued at over £1 million.

(iii) Computer design development to facilitate initial costings, knife-making, computer-stitching programmes and trouble-free manufacture. Pictured Russell Munton.

(iv) A section of the clicking room where the uppers are cut and (v) a close up of John Riches using the press on the knives.

(vi) Preparation of the uppers (Michael Plunkett) and (vii) the 'bottom stuff' (Douglas Barr) before (viii) colour marking (Lea Young).

(i)

(ii)

(iii)

(iv)

(v)

(vi)

(vii)

(viii)

(ix)

(x)

(xi)

(xii)

(xiii)

(xiv)

(xv)

(xvi)

(ix) Jackie Burrows and Sandra Billman working in one of the closing rooms where hundreds of skilled machinists stitch the uppers together and trim and decorate them.

(x) The uppers are then lasted and (xi) the 'bottom stuff' attached by sophisticated machinery controlled by operatives working with skill and precision. Pictured John Martin and Dennis Lubbock.

(xii) And on to the shoe room where handling blemishes in manufacture are removed, (xiii) an inspection is carried out and the shoes boxed. Pictured Kim Stapley.

(xiv) Co-operation between the sales office staff (pictured here) and the warehouse staff ensures that retailers get the shoes quickly.

(xv) A section of the Start-rite computer staff whose work involves every aspect of shoemaking today.

(xvi) Judy Dawe, advertising manager and Carol Brown, checking the loading of the portable stand for the Spring Shoe Show at the NEC, Birmingham.

The Start-rite sales team photographed at the NEC Spring Shoe Fair with Mike Hull (sales director) and Michael Chesworth (joint managing director).

The Board in session (left to right): Roger Hook (production), Mike Hull (sales), John Church (non-executive), David White (chairman and joint managing director), Michael Chesworth (joint managing director), Mike Hodkinson (director and general manager Domani Retail), Peter Lamble (financial director).

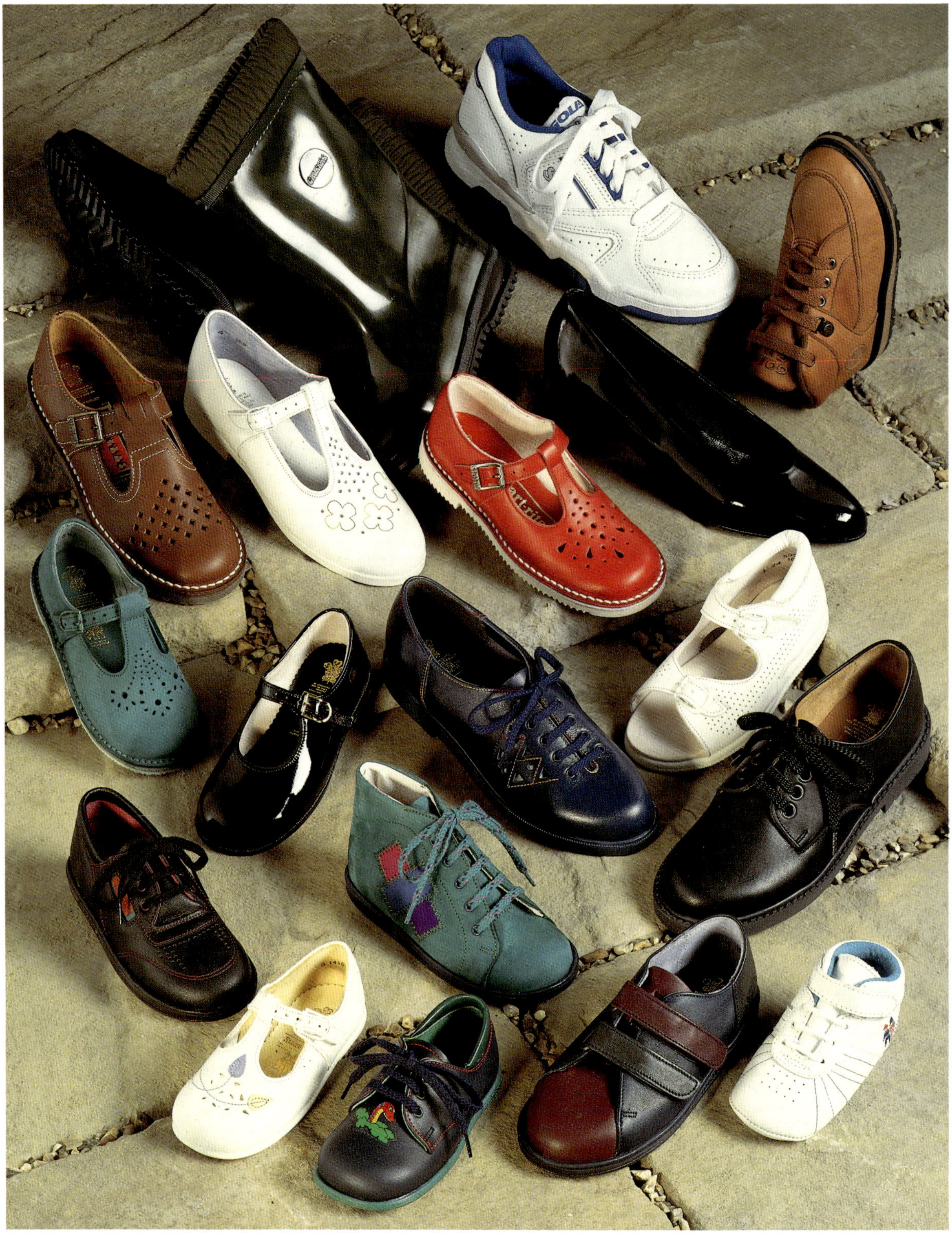

A selection of styles from the 1992 Start-rite collection illustrate the wide variety of footwear available in this leading brand today.

more to the investment of profits in on-going development — a strategy that has kept the company afloat for 200 years.

A time for important decisions

The eighty-fifth annual meeting of the company, held in October 1984, was the last one attended by James Hanly. He was in failing health and David White was effectively in control of group policy, although he was not appointed group chairman until the following year, after his uncle's death.

The board was strengthened by the appointment as a non-executive director of John Church, managing director and vice-chairman of Church & Co. plc, one of the most consistently successful shoe manufacturing companies in the country, and chairman of its retail company A. Jones & Sons. Before entering the shoe industry John Church qualified as a chartered accountant and had worked as a management consultant.

John Church's sound judgement, wide business experience, and ability to ask pertinent and awkward questions, has been a great help in deciding company policy in recent years.

With new plant and equipment being continually introduced and the stringent control of output based on a realistic assessment of the potential market, shoes were being produced even more economically with the accent still on the use of top-grade leathers and materials and top quality throughout.

It was proving to be the right policy and, with the birth-rate rising again, there was what financial journalists always describe as 'cautious optimism' ahead. There still was not stability throughout the industry — there seldom is — and there remained some serious changes taking place demanding long and careful study at Crome Road.

Among the most important was the relentless change taking place in shoe retailing and the serious fall in the number of independent retailers. This was because their profits were inadequate for many of them to maintain good staffing levels to pay the increased rents and rates on prime shopping sites. The more cheap, imported shoes they sold compounded their problems. Also property values rose, making it attractive to sell their property and live instead on invested money.

Between 1977 and 1987 it was estimated that multiple retailers had increased their share of all sales to 75 per cent. Start-rite's 1,000 or so independent retailers, many of them customers for many decades, were decreasing at a rate which could not be ignored.

The strategic decision was taken to continue to support and encourage the independent retailer, while making every effort to increase sales to those top-grade multiple customers who had turned their backs on the growing custom of people selecting their own shoes in the shops, and were willing to offer a service of trained fitters in their children's department. The diminishing number of independents, of whom only a limited number were able to trade in prime shopping areas, left Start-rite no alternative.

The difficulties of much of the retail trade remained. To improve survival prospects Start-rite — exasperated by the reticence of others — embarked on a policy aimed at increasing profitability for retailers selling their products. Mark-ups and trading terms were increased to levels still not matched by other manufacturers in their product sector. It was widely welcomed by retailers, and vast numbers have seen profits from the sale of Start-rite products reach levels that have sustained their business during difficult times, and allowed them to develop and strengthen their business during the good times.

Considerable effort was made by the sales team and others to bring home the advantages of trading with Start-rite. Their hard work met with rewarding success. Simultaneously, the relentless policy of striving for top-quality shoemaking, using the best of leathers and materials available, masterminded by Michael Chesworth, and carried out by Roger Hook and his staff, began to pay dividends, 'literally and metaphorically' as the chairman expressed it at the time.

Once more bucking the trend in the British industry for home-produced footwear, sales figures went up again, creating seventy new production jobs in 1988 and once more allowing what has been the centuries-old company policy of ploughing back a large part of the profits to be revived.

Investment was maintained at a high level, with specific targets being data processing, customer service, production technology and the expansion of Domani Retail.

Part of the Domani shop at Cardiff after reopening last year.

Michael Chesworth, joint managing director.

A new name, Domani — 'tomorrow' in Italian — was gradually becoming widely recognised as a fashionable shoe for older children and teenagers, made by Start-rite with all the quality, fitting and other plus factors of the brand. For a child's first shoes, and for younger children, Start-rite was still the first choice of parents and children, although the age at which girls become fashion-conscious, and demanded shoes like their mother or elder sister, was becoming younger and younger. Hence, Domani and its successful advertising theme, 'reflections of fashion'.

For the same compelling reason the name of the First Footing shops was changed to Domani, with additional shops being opened in areas where there was a demand for Start-rite shoes not being covered by retailers. Gradually, the shops were refurbished, and the windows and décor made attractive to potential Domani customers, as well as parents and young children, often through the departments being separated.

General manager, Michael Hodkinson, and his team worked hard to make a success of Domani Retail, and gradually succeeded. Once more the never-ending difficulties and disappointments which are endemic in the British shoe trade had been overcome by teamwork throughout the company.

Meeting the challenge ahead

During the latter years of the 1980s shoe manufacturing in Britain remained a precarious business, with imports, benefiting from a strong pound sterling, growing relentlessly.

For Start-rite there was only one route for survival — the creation of a knowledgeable specialist management in all areas. It was recognised that the days had long gone when the Charles Winters and the James Southalls could successfully run a business employing close on 1,000 people on an autocratic basis.

In the autumn of 1988 Michael Chesworth was appointed joint managing director with David White, who continued as chairman. His responsibilities were defined as marketing, sales and the company's retail group, with the chairman taking responsibility for finance, management services and production.

No one, said the chairman, had worked more enthusiastically, effectively, or longer hours for the group than Michael Chesworth. His consistent — and insistent — marketing policy of lifting the quality of Start-rite footwear to yet higher levels in design and materials had received a ready response from retail stockists and the public.

So, 1988 was a marvellous year for the company, with the law which says that if anything can go wrong in business it will do so, miraculously held in suspension. There was a group increase in sales of 25 per cent shared between home and overseas sales, and the Domani Retail company.

The popularity of the newly-developed Gola SRi leisure-trainer range added further impetus to sales, in tandem with a significant increase in Norwich-made styles.

Another factor was that the improvements to the computer control of stock under the new system masterminded by Chris Speake, was speeding up the rate at which stock was turning over in the warehouse. It was realised that this most necessary provision, with its automatic bar-coding facility for reordering by retailers, enabling them to carry smaller stocks, was highly likely to lead to smaller initial orders.

Experience has shown that at times this is indeed happening, but overall, the fact that Start-rite was the first shoe manufacturer to offer customers electronic equipment for stock control has paid dividends for both customer and company.

Another first at this time, which gained Start-rite an accolade in the trade press, and commendations by their many customers specialising in fitting, was the introduction of a sixth width fitting for children's shoes. It might have been thought that in the leisurely days of motor-cars and buses everywhere that children's feet would have become smaller over the years. Not a bit of it.

The policy of keeping watch on children's feet, and constantly updating the survey, made it plain that there was a demand for an 'H' fitting, wider than the five existing ones, so the necessary investment in research and last-making was allocated, and ahead of the opposition, the 'H' fitting became available. It now sells regularly more pairage than the narrowest 'C' fitting.

The beginning of 1989 got off to the best of all possible starts by the award of the Royal Warrant of Appointment as Shoemakers to the Prince of Wales. It replaced the Royal Warrant granted by the Queen in 1955 for supplying shoes to the then Duke of Cornwall and Princess Anne. With the Queen's children now with children of their own, the new appointment recognised the continuation of the excellence of Start-rite footwear.

There followed a magnificent eighteen months. The Royal Appointment was succeeded by Start-rite being chosen by the Independent Footwear Retailers' Association as the top manufacturer of the year. When the IFRA president, Roger Clinkard, announced the award winners at the Café Royal dinner in London, it came as a great surprise to many of those present, because many of the independent shops represented there did not sell children's shoes and were therefore unlikely to have voted for Start-rite.

Michael Chesworth acknowledged that the win came as a surprise because Start-rite supplied only a part of the retailers' product requirements and by no means all of the IFRA members. The award, he said, was a tribute to the work of the sales force, and to those who worked so diligently in Norwich to make the high-quality product so greatly appreciated by more and more retailers.

It was yet another indication that after a period of intense critical self-

MODERN TIMES

examination the company was getting things right. There was more to come. Start-rite won the prestigious Barclays Bank Business of the Year Award, sponsored by the *Eastern Daily Press*. For a shoe manufacturer to win this award in competition with all other businesses at that particular time was generally unexpected and was a clear indication of the bankers' approval of the way the company was run, as well as its product.

The judges were quoted as saying that it was the top company because of being healthy, well managed and forward-looking, and, above all, because it had thoroughly researched its needs in combating cheap imports.

Now, as the actual bicentenary date approaches, and this book has to get off to the printer if it is to be delivered on time, the country's economy is once more severely depressed, with rising unemployment and less money for people to buy the things they need, even such essentials as fitting footwear for their children.

But still the good news continued. The Independent Footwear Retailers' Association again chose Start-rite as manufacturer of the year, and autumn and winter sales were ahead of the previous year.

Michael Chesworth, joint managing director, presents to Debbie Pengilly, manageress of Domani at Debenhams, Plymouth the merit shield of Domani Retail which she won for the second time in succession. Also in the picture is Maureen Parfitt, manageress of Domani Retail, Woking.

TWO CENTURIES OF SHOEMAKING: START-RITE 1792-1992

Roger Hook (top left), production director, and Michael Hull (top right), sales director, who are chairmen of the production and development, and sales and services divisions respectively.

Members of the four operational divisions created under the decentralised new management structure. (Centre, from left to right) Quentin Stevens, sales manager independent accounts; Peter Cross, sales manager multiple accounts; Harry Meekings, director of design and development; and Mike Tassie, director of planning. (Below, from left to right) Chris Speake, director of services; Graham Cox, director of operations; Peter Lamble, financial director; and Mike Baxter, director of buying.

Despite the problems of a growing recession, 1990 was a solidly profitable year for the company through efficient stock control, management of cash-flow and the encouraging performance of the Domani Retail company. While the management of cash-flow involved a careful look at all outgoings, it did not mean a lack of investment for the future. A heavy investment was made to employ additional highly qualified and experienced men and women in important jobs in middle management, all but one of them in areas where the jobs had not existed previously.

A strategy document, *New Management Structures for the 1990s*, was published, and its implementation begun. Within it is the means to involve all employees in the future of the company.

Group management has been decentralised and restructured into four operational divisions — sales and services, production and development, central, and retail. The new structure utilises to the full the skills inherent in senior and middle management, with great benefit to all. The number of employees on profit share is being expanded rapidly. Each divisional management board is responsible, under the leadership of the board director in charge, for the company's performance in their particular area of operations.

Plans to ensure Start-rite's long-term future into the twenty-first century are already being finalised, but they are hardly likely to be announced yet, nor even those for the concluding years of this century.

What is certain is that Start-rite is determined to continue to provide the best shoes of the highest quality with the most efficient service to customers. The aim will be to achieve it by on-going investment in all aspects of the company's operations, but particularly in people, training and plant, combined with the retention of the centuries-old proven practice of stringent financial control.

Produced by:
Publicity Plus Ltd, Norwich and London

Photographs by:
GGS Photo Graphics, Norwich
Front cover, pages 68, 104

Eastern Counties Newspapers, Norwich
Pages 16, 66, 109

Alan Howard
Pages 9, 55, 56, 57, 58, 77, 78, 101, 102, 103, 107, 110

Jacqueline Wyatt
Inside front cover

Philip Gammon
Page 79

Post Studios Ltd, Birmingham
Page 103

Bateman Studios, Cardiff
Page 106

Additional photography by
John Howell of Start-rite

Designed by:
Jane Martin

Typeset by:
Norfolk Origination Services, Norwich

Printed by:
Norwich Colour Print Ltd, Norwich

Bound by:
J W Braithwaite and Son Ltd, Wolverhampton